Introduction

My husband, Charlie, was diagnosed with multiple sclerosis when he was 34. Immediately after diagnosis and during the last two years of his life Charlie made his feelings about MS public through his writing. His column in *The Independent on Sunday* started in 2001 and over a decade later he began his blog, 'Dying for Beginners'. Charlie kept posting blog entries until just before he died, at the end of January 2016.

These diaries chart, I hope, the lowest periods of Charlie's life. I know of no worse. They were the worst times for me too: our adult lives were completely intertwined. We met when we were both 19. Whatever happened to him happened to me too, to a greater or lesser extent, and vice versa. Just as with any long, close relationship.

'Going public' was not my style at all. Charlie wrote about our lives – his, mine, the children's – on his terms, not mine. I have barely edited his words, which is why, save for the last two entries, which Charlie dictated to me, as 'Dying for Beginners' progresses, there are more punctuation and grammar 'mistakes' and the formatting becomes more ragged. This reflects Charlie's deterioration. For that, read my deterioration too.

So why am I publishing 'Dying for Beginners'? First, this was Charlie's repeated wish during his final years. He longed to see his blog turned into a book.

Second, after Charlie died, the head of the Multiple Sclerosis International Federation (MSIF), Peer Baneke, wrote to me:

> Charlie's blog was an inspiration for me, firing me on to do my work as best I can. This cannot always have been easy to read for you. He wrote with such ruthless honesty. Sometimes I thought, "Charlie, you can't write this in a blog". You must have loved him very much to let him be himself in that respect. With all the pain, realism, ridicule, hope and despair – and through his harshness, the love for you and for your children – what he wrote rang always very true. My father had MS, and I recognised so much of all that happens around MS, not only to him, but to my mother, my brothers and sisters, and to the relations between us all. Charlie dared to write about all that.

Finally, I like to think I was granted a kind of poetic licence. Charlie's sister, Candy, contacted the poet John Hegley, of whom Charlie was a huge fan, to ask if he had written a pug poem that could be read out at the funeral. He hadn't, despite being a fellow pug lover, but immediately wrote one, although Charlie was a stranger to him.

When I asked John Hegley if I might publish 'Charlie's' pug poem in this book, he replied yes instantly, adding: "As you have sensed, his blog is of value to the world." Charlie would have disagreed, and claimed not to care if people gained nothing from

Charlie, Martha, Rory, Lucy and Daisy in Suffolk, July 2012

his words, but on this one, I'm siding with the poet instead of my husband. Thank you, John Hegley, you're a kind and funny man.

Charlie was kind and funny too, and watching him die was absolutely awful. There were times when neither of us behaved well. If you read between the lines, it isn't hard to find blog entries where we were at odds, or had had a row. But we also laughed a lot. Charlie always tried to crack a joke, even when at the end, when he could barely speak.

I have no idea what the meaning of life is. Charlie claimed to hate the idea that all this suffering gave either of us any special wisdom, but to be kind and to laugh seem important to me (and when you have a temper like mine, this can be a terrible challenge). And don't bank on second chances, do all you can now. Or, in the words of an inscription I once saw above an almshouse in Southwold: 'Be kind quickly'.

When Charlie was alive and a new blog entry appeared in my in-box, sometimes I wouldn't read it for hours, dreading his latest report on the chaos at home. Now, of course, I cherish everything Charlie wrote, including 'Dying for Beginners'. Now he has gone, Charlie's writing is amongst my most treasured possessions.

Lucy Alexander
Cambridge, January 2017

Contents

Foreword by David Dimbleby

I first met Charlie when he became editor of *Question Time*, the weekly political programme I present for the BBC. We became firm friends. I soon realised that the key to understanding Charlie was to realise that he did everything at speed. He thought fast, he spoke fast, he wrote fast and read fast. He fizzed with new ideas about everything, from how politics should be conducted to how television programmes, not just his but all television programmes, could be improved, or better still reinvented. He was, at least to outward appearances, supremely confident in his own abilities. I asked him once, after he had been away for a week at home in Essex, what he had been doing. "Oh. I've written a novel" he said airily. "In a week?" I asked incredulously. "Oh yes" he said, "nothing to it. You just sit down and write." He had, I later discovered, read a book called *How to Write a Novel* – and that was that.

Charlie's impatience with anybody and anything that stood in his way could have been irritating but was, in reality, stimulating and enjoyable, if exhausting. He was funny and endearing, and loved by those who knew him.

For someone with such energy, such individuality, such a passion for doing the unexpected, for going his own way, to be struck down with multiple sclerosis was a particularly vicious blow. His whole life was about communication, but the ability to communicate was gradually and cruelly withdrawn from him. Speaking became harder and writing reduced to one shaky finger, struggling to spell words out on his keyboard.

When he was first diagnosed, he decided to go public about his illness. He published 120 blogs and many articles about his physical and mental state, and how his life and his life with his family was affected. As you will discover as you read this thoughtful and moving account, he never asks for sympathy, let alone pity. He is often funny and always perceptive. As he himself said: "This dying thing is really quite interesting" and he was right.

David Dimbleby
December 2016

Cast

Family
Long-suffering wife/L-SW – Lucy
Slavey – Daisy
Too-cool-for-school – Martha
Climb-anything Son – Rory

Medical
E – Ed, old friend who introduced Charlie to the stem cell trial
G – Giles, Charlie's former neurologist in Essex
J – mostly Judith, our GP, although there are other Js
M – Mary, Charlie's MS Nurse
R – Rob, old friend and brother-in-law of E
TGC / The Great Compston – Professor Alastair Compston, CBE, FRS, Professor
Emeritus of Neurology, Department of Clinical Neurosciences, University of
Cambridge

Work
DD – David Dimbleby (Godfather of climb-anything son)
DF – Sir David Frost
JSP – Janet Street Porter, editor of *The Independent on Sunday* when Charlie worked there
S – Sue Douglas, editor of *people.co.uk*, where dying for beginners was first published
Sindy/Sindie – *The Independent on Sunday*
SoC – Sarah, friend and former colleague at Al Jazeera

Places
Swotsville – Cambridge, Charlie started writing his blog just after we moved here
– and apologies to the county of Suffolk and people who don't work in TV.

Charlie Courtauld

Dying for Beginners

2013

00
Monday 26 August

I am dying. Nothing unusual there; we all are − sometime. And I won't die of my MS – few people do. It's not categorised as a fatal disease.

No, I won't die of MS. But I probably will die soon, and it'll be some trivial thing which gets me – <u>something which wouldn't have done if I didn't have MS</u>. Some infection, some fall, starvation, whatever.

I don't do misery memoirs. I produce TV. It's part of my self-definition. Asked to describe myself in five ways, making TV programmes – like *Question Time* or David Frost's stuff for Al-Jazeera – that would be there, along with 'left-handed' and 'smoker'.

But my left hand's gone. And I keep dropping fags in this bloody wheelchair. So it's all change. I'm 47. Not too young, not too old. The end should be decades away. I don't want to die, nor leave my wife a widow or deprive my kids of a dad. But it's gonna happen anyway, I fear.

Let's get one thing straight right at the start. Or two things, actually. I want to make them absolutely clear:
1. I'm not brave
2. I'm not wise, either.

Ever since that Job bloke came out in all those stinky pustules, and suffered and became an even holier prophet or whatever, these two saws have been embedded in our consciousness:
1. People find some sort of bravery in suffering
2. People find some sort of other-earthly wisdom in suffering.
Crap.

Pain is just painful. Humiliation is just humiliating. Fear is just frightening.
But what they aren't is boring. This dying thing is really quite interesting. Sad, but interesting.

So don't call me wise. Don't call me brave. Just call me curious.

01 More than one, fewer than five.

Thursday 29 August

People's reaction to my prognosis is unpredictable. Some like to seize on the first three words. More than one year, that's plenty of time. So you aren't dying today, tomorrow, or anytime soon. Get busy living.

Others focus on the last three words. Five years max? Nightmare! Poor you. Get busy dying. Dying – particularly of the slowish kind – is something that people find hard to get a handle on. More than a year, fewer than five. So many questions, so few answers. Am I going too fast, or too slow? Will it hurt? Should I buy life insurance? Is there any point in giving up smoking?

These, and many more of the questions about death I intend to explore over the coming weeks. I find them interesting: I hope you will too.

It's going to happen to everyone you know and everyone you don't. Everyone who has ever lived and everyone who ever will. Your parents, your siblings, your children – even your great-great grandchildren.

And, of course, its going to happen to you. Maybe tomorrow. Maybe on the 23rd of October 2021 at 7.37am.

But it's something we prefer not to think about. 'It's morbid,' we are told. Fairly obvious that, but so what? Or 'it's pointless'. Yes, well, so is thinking about winning the lottery; but that doesn't stop anyone.

But the mysterious and hidden nature of death has led to a vast plethora of nonsense. To take just one example: 'There are more people alive today than have ever died.' Or 'The living outnumber the dead'. Or 'The planet's current population is greater than the sum of all the people in our history who have lived and died.' Whichever way you say it, it is an absolutely stunning 'fact'; one which I have heard repeated by government ministers in the House of Commons, on the Today Programme, in broadsheet newspapers, even in pop lyrics. Once heard, never forgotten.

And it isn't true. Not by a long way – a factor of thirty, perhaps. Only those who believe that human life began with Adam and Eve in 2004 BC can give credence to this oft-repeated and widely-believed mantra.

But nonsense is a fairly common feature when dealing with death. We don't understand it; we don't discuss it.

It's going to happen only once to all of us. There are no second tries or best-of-threes. So we don't want to mess it up. And for me, it is a very immediate issue. Thanks to this bloody MS, I am dying. Not immediately: more than a year. But fewer than five. And I want to get it right. Join me as I find out about this thing.

02 Will it hurt?
Monday 28 October

I'm writing now on my way to South Africa to make a programme for Al Jazeera English. I'm in hellish pain right now – 4 bad falls today and I think I might have cracked a rib, it's so sore. But nothing, nothing is going to stop me from making this trip.

I am a TV producer. That's what I do. Make TV. When I used to work at the BBC, I ran *Question Time*. Now I've ended up at Al Jazeera, and I've organised a sort of QT-lite for them. Cool location, cool panel. Cool.

Not only that, but they've sent out a 'carer' with me, and Nick will help in any way. Like showing me where to eat. Or buying me fags. Or taking cool photos of me looking moody.

But it still doesn't answer the question. And none of my panelists, however old – Jimmy Carter, or godly – Desmond Tutu, can. Because none of them has died, yet. Soon, maybe. But by then I can't ask them.

The programmes are made. They went well. Shows like this are all about timing and stopwatches: 3 words a second, 12 minutes a question. Despite the weather. I'd been told that there's only about 3 days of rain a year over here. If that's right, I was here for every one of them. The panel were pretty much as expected: Jimmy Carter a bore, Desmond Tutu lovely etc, and they all agreed with each other too much.

So will it hurt? There are, of course, painful things that can make you die. Getting your throat slit or drinking bleach must hurt like hell. But that doesn't make the dying bit painful. And I doubt it is. What would be the point?

So will it hurt? Probably not.

03 What is it?
Wednesday 6 November

What is it? There doesn't seem to be an awful lot of point in me banging on about death without a clear definition of what it is. So here goes: "Death is…." Um.

The trouble is, there isn't one. We all know what it isn't – life. But even my great guru, Wikipedia – doesn't seem to quite know what it is.

Wikipedia, by the way, has an unjustifiably toxic reputation. Almost every student of journalism I have interviewed in the last decade thinks that I will be impressed if they assert that Wikipedia is off-limits for researching a story.

They don't get the job. Wikipedia is amazing. Along, maybe with Shazam, its the best thing about the internet. Yes, it sometimes gets it wrong. Yes, you do have to check. But blimey. I can write a ten-minute interview in about five minutes, thanks to Wikipedia.

But I digress. It looks like there are two definitions. Brain death (end of consciousness) and the ending of heartbeat and breathing. Pretty flaky stuff. I'd always assumed that death was momentary – one second you're alive, the next you aren't. But it's less clear than that. All those people 'brought back?' I'd always assumed that they weren't dead really, that they were just deluded. But maybe they were dead. And then they weren't. Damn.

Add the word 'irreversible' to your definition and you're getting somewhere. But how do you know if something is irreversible until you've tried?

04 Railway Children
Sunday 10 November

The Railway Children? Jenny Agutter running through the steam crying 'Daddy, oh my daddy?' That's ok. So is Lassie, just about. But *Elf? Miss Congeniality? Legally Blonde? Up?* Oh, come on.

One of the more annoying, irritating, symptoms of this MS is called 'inappropriate emotional response.' Put simply, it means that I roar with giggles at the only mildly amusing – and blub like a baby at mawkish Hollywood pap.

For my kids in particular, this is hugely shaming. Not only is their dad in a wheelchair, which guarantees crummy seats at the movies, but he then tends, rather loudly, to howl at the flick.

It rather limits my outings. Last year, my wife wanted to see a classical piano concert. The sight and sound of that pompous man in a tailcoat set me off. He played, I laughed. He played louder. I laughed louder. Everyone looked round and tutted.

I know that I wouldn't have behaved like this before. So the essential question is: is this the real me? More honest, seeing through pompous piano playing? Or an easily-manipulated cretin, putty in Hollywood's glitz? And, is *Miss Congeniality* really that good? All of which makes this dying business even harder to get a handle on. If I'm not the same 'me' I was, or would have been, has that person already 'died'?

05
Saturday 16 November

We went for a walk by the river this morning. I say 'walk', but it wasn't, of course. I was in my buggy, Long-Suffering Wife and Climb-anything Son had bikes, and the dog was on a lead. I hardly burned up the calories, but it was lovely to be out by the Cam. Then to the cashpoint on the way home, to get out some dosh for a haircut, which seems to cost a bloomin' packet these days. The buggy made it, thank goodness. It's fairly awful when it doesn't and I need to be pushed home by Long-Suffering Wife. That happened only yesterday, when I paid the price of a detour to look round the Fitzwilliam museum. So, should I fork out for a replacement battery, which will set me back by yet another hundred?

Money. Cash. Dosh, Wonga. It's yet another worry when you're sick. And when you're not, I guess. But in one way, the solution is clearer from my position. I simply need it, and soon. Staying with my parents here in Essex while building continues in Cambridge, I just dropped and broke my second iPad in a month. I've never had a reliable grip. But with all feeling gone in my left hand now, I drop even more than ever. And Apple products aren't cheap.

My family are probably gonna need money for longer than me. For some bizarre reason I don't even qualify for free prescriptions − and I take a lot of pills. It's only 10am now, and I've already had three! I got rejected for life insurance the other day. Not a surprise, I guess. But it was still a shock, I must confess.

The MS society told me about some Swiss fools who might offer me a ridiculously good bet. After all the banker-bashing of recent months, I had assumed that they are all just floppy-haired dimwits drawing 200% bonuses who would be only too glad to insure me. It turns out that nobody's that stupid. Not even Fred the Shred types, it appears. It's often portrayed as selfless, generous, life insurance. For some people, I'm sure it is, saving while you can for a future you won't see. But not for me. It was a totally selfish act. The idea of leaving my wife lonely AND poor is a torment for me; the thought that she will be an impoverished widow at 50 is hideous. The prospect of fixing either made me feel a lot less awful. Getting a way out seemed a total bargain; being turned down was like adding insult to injury. Another reason to loathe Switzerland.

06 Have I lost the plot?
Sunday 17 November

One of the less thrillsome things about this disease is that you can get very muddled thinking. And your memory goes. All of which may mean that I am no longer me – if you get me.

So off to hospital for a psychological assessment. It was in a broom cupboard with lots of handy shelves, but no natural light.

I had to look at some faces, and recall them later. I had to read a list of oddly-pronounced words, like 'demesne' or 'campanile'. I had to remember a long boring story about a burglar with a scar.

I reckon I did ok. But I also am certain that I would have done better six months ago. The nice young woman psychologist thinks I may be 'wallowing in death', whatever that means.

After a couple of days, the report. Not much of a surprise to me, but still a bit of a shock to have it in writing. I'm good on the weird words, bog-standard on the burglar, disastrous on the faces. In the bottom 5% of the population.

Remembering people has never been a strong point, but now it's official – and even has a number: <5%.

I was called in again to Addenbrooke's the other day, but it was cancelled at the last minute, so I had to buggy half an hour all the way home again. The buggy's battery just made it. At some point it'll go flat in the middle of nowhere and strand me. But not yet, thank goodness. This would be a bad time, Christmas AND builders.

07
Monday 18 November

We've got the builders in. For the next month they will be digging, shaping ramps, fashioning a wet room. When it's all done, I will be able to live a downstairs existence, and never again have face those steep stairs. So we've stocked up on coffee and tea and those pink biscuits which only builders eat.

But there's a worry. Why should we spend any excess lolly on adaptations which may only be temporary, and impoverish my wife and kids in the process? The answer is obvious – the doctors MAY have got it wrong; I may have decades left. And these adaptations will make my time – however long – more do-able.

But still. It's a poser. Our middle daughter is fretting about it. She frets about everything these days. Not good for a 15 year-old. She was always so happy-go-lucky. We all were. In some ways I'd like to protect them all from this thing. But I can't. Our 12 year-old son has to pick me up off the floor when I fall, and our 17 year-old eldest daughter uncomplainingly sweeps up my multiple broken cups.

And for the next month I have to leave the house anyway and move back to Essex with my parents, while wife and kids stay. That's a pain, too. My folks are great. They've got a new wheelchair I can use in Essex which can turn like nothing I've seen before. And my uncle has made a wooden ramp so I can get about the house. But they didn't expect – or want – one of their kids to be such a worry. This is their time to be looked after, by me. Not the other way.

All of which adds to the burden on my wife. If it's no fun being the ill person, it's no fun being married to one, either. Whenever we argue, usually on Saturdays, the argument usually ends with me falling over. How can you win an argument like that? Not a fair fight.

08
Monday 25 November

Cranks…Well-meaning but misguided types, or evil bastards sponging of the weakness of the poorly, depending on your viewpoint. But the upshot is the same – a lot of money wasted and a lot of disappointment.

For an accident of numbers – a lot of patients, unpredictable outcomes, no useful treatments, long-term illness – the disease I have, MS, attracts cranks like a cow pat does flies. Someone is going to make a bloody fortune out of this thing, if they can only stumble on the cure. And they're trying.

And patients like me will try anything. Believe me, over the past decade, I've given many of them a shot. Dope, oxygen tanks, anti-diarrhoea pills, homeopathic drops, rescue remedy, vitamin D jabs. I even had all my mercury fillings out, at the behest of a kindly godmother, and replaced. I injected myself every day for seven years, until I was so bruised that it hurt like hell to lie in bed.

But none of it made any discernible difference. Most people's first experiences of MS is of a relapsing-remitting kind, where symptoms suddenly come and equally suddenly go. I lost my sense of taste, twice, for months and it then returned. That's just what happens.

No offence – or not much anyway – to those lovely (credulous) folk who believe in one or another of the quack remedies. I would just say the magic words 'randomised double-blind placebo trial' and most of them go away. But, if I said a mouthful like that, I might need a lie-down too.

Drug trials are, theoretically, great. But one-third of trial patients are on placebo sugar pills. And another third are on the real stuff – but at the wrong dose. Only a lucky, randomly chosen few are getting the right amount of the potion.

All that doesn't stop us from trying. I was on the cannabis drug trial a few years ago. I had a little laminated card. To flash at the cops if they tried to bust me and break my front door down at 3.00am, saying that the Home Secretary was allowing me to possess and use marijuana. But I reckoned I was on the placebo with no effect whatever, and I wasn't allowed to drive, so I pulled out.

Because that's what the cranks really fear; not hot-blooded emotion – there's plenty of that about when you're dealing with disease. Not, it's cool, cold-blooded science and statistics which gets them running. All sorts of excuses will suddenly appear, a long-winded reason why this particular brand of snake oil – stinging nettles on a full moon, or whatever – isn't suitable for scientific study. Balls. Any brand which refuses to be tested is cobblers. And you can test that theory.

09

Sunday 1 December

Holiday in Morocco. Five days away from kids and builders. Should be relaxing, peaceful. But it can't be. Not with me in a buggy, and all the pressure on Long-Suffering Wife to make this fun, memorable, because it may, just may, be our last holiday together. And compulsory fun is no fun.

Marrakesh is lovely, bustling, colourful. But steps are an integral part of Arab architecture and, like a Dalek, I can't do steps. Even the pavements are a foot high. My buggy is well-travelled: this is its third trip to Africa, and British Airways are quite used to it by now. So getting it here is no problem. More of a problem is getting about. Or it would be, without the helpful Moroccans, who make up for steps and kerbs by carrying my buggy – which weighs a ton – up and down every obstacle, with only a single fag for payment.

But noise and bustle, colour and mopeds and gratitude to strangers tend to wear you down after couple of days. And we might need our energy soon. So we've come to these mountains for a couple of days. Wife is climbing the mountain opposite, and I'm lazing with wifi and iPad down here. Perfect.

10 Fags
Friday 20 December

"I could give up smoking any time. I've done it five times already!" It's an old joke, but in my case there's an element of truth in it. Ever since the ban on tabbing indoors came in, I've given up for 3 months every year, preferring not to go outdoors into pissing rain and freezing wind. For those terrible weeks every year, I switch to snuff, which is horrid, makes my nose run like a tap, but is very, very cheap – certainly compared to fags, which cost – to coin a phrase – a packet.

It's also a test of my willpower, of course. The very fact that I CAN stub it out means – to my muddled thinking, at least – that I COULD if I ever have to; if the reds invade and force their horrid unfiltered commie butts on us. Nonsense, of course. I'm sure I would never manage it. I just hope I'll never have to find out.

I've been a smoker for decades now. It's become a part of my self-definition. I drop lit fags all the time nowadays, and I have to use an unfamiliar (right) hand. But fag in hand, I can forget any worries for a while, and it still feels like all is well.

Lunch today with old friends from way back in my Week in Politics days. When I started in TV, you could light up in the office. And I did; even Hansard every day was a pleasure to read, given sufficient cigarettes and coffee. So appalled by my filthy habit was our presenter, Vincent Hanna, that he bet me £1,000 that I couldn't give up for a week. A fool and his money were soon parted.

Within a few months of my habit starting, back in the 80s, UK tobacconists stopped selling my chosen brand, John Player Blue. It was great; ever since then, I have had no brand loyalty, flitting from one type of fag to another. Today I'm on Marlboro Lights – the last of my Duty Frees from Morocco. Tomorrow? Who knows, who cares? Silk Cut, probably.

There aren't that many advantages to my circumstances, but this is one. Smoking is a freebie for me. There's not much doubt that this habit will cut my life expectancy – or it would if that expectancy was normal. Now that risk has shrivelled, trumped by this MS.

Humans are notoriously bad with probability, chance, risk. Even that board game; I never can remember whether Yakutsk is north of Irkutsk or vice versa. And I was never much good at Maths, but even I can see that if smoking takes five years off my life expectancy, and this disease takes thirty, then lighting up probably won't damage anything but my bank balance.

Long-Suffering Wife is exasperated by this stubbornness. I know that it sets a crappy example for the kids. Middle girl, Too-Cool-for-School – only fifteen – is already at it, we suspect. My lighters keep disappearing, and she always seems well-stocked when I need to light a bonfire.

Sorry everyone. Got to go. It's lighting-up time.

2014

11 Panto
Saturday 25 January

It's panto time. Oh no it isn't. Oh yes it is etc. I know that most places have done their pantos by Twelfth night, but things are different up here in North Essex. End of Jan/beginning of Feb is a fairly normal time for us.

I was in the village pantomime for years. It got me – and the kids – out of the house and away from stage frightened Long-Suffering Wife for a few hours of rehearsal every winter Wednesday. Now because we have builders in Cambridge – and have had to move out – I am back at the panto, not as a participant, but in the audience.

They've become more professional since I left. There's even a website, (www.ceds.org. uk), and there are halfway decent prizes in the raffle this year. But it's still the same old CEDs [Colne Engaine Dramatic Society]: beautiful set, forgotten lines and all.

It's behind you. Oh no it isn't. Oh yes it is etc. The last time these people saw me I could – in a panto manner – dance and sing. I've done many things: Friar Tuck, Robinson Crusoe, Ogre, Dame… usually a baddie, but not a really bad one. The one who dies by the end of Act 1 (and so doesn't have so many lines to learn). Now I'm in this chair 24/7 and my voice is little more than a whisper. There is no way that I could perform in anything now.

This is the first time they've seen me since my health fell off a cliff back in September. Fairly shocking, but it was well-disguised. No mention of the chair. All hail-fellow-well-met chumminess. Like I'd never been away. I guess that's good. But what can people say? What do I want to hear?

Three wishes. Because there's the rub about this chair. I really don't – in my heart of hearts – associate it with ME. I think of it as temporary, really useful, fantastic. But I secretly think that one day my wish will be granted, and I'll be walking and running again, that the wicked witch's spell will soon be broken, I will sweep L-SW off her feet and we'll get a one-way ticket to happily ever after.

Chick chick chick chick chicken, lay a little egg for me. They say that panto is a very British phenomenon. All that rather spooky men-dressed-as-women and girls-as-principal-boy stuff. But everyone, everywhere loves a fairy tale and this is one: Grimm.

12 A9
Saturday 15 February

Last year I got a speeding ticket on the A9 near Inverness. Today, Long-Suffering Wife got stopped by Scots police on the same stretch – this time for an illegal overtake while we were all singing along to a Magnetic Fields track. But my dislike of this road – the 'spine of Scotland' – has almost nothing to do with the last 3 points on my old licence or the impending three points to come on L-SW's.

It is a horrible, slow, road works-filled crawl from Falkirk to Inverness and beyond. At least I was allowed to drive a year ago. And at least I could go fast enough to get 3 points! Now I'm relegated to the passenger seat and there's a flipping wheelchair in the back. But some things don't change. The A9 is still a queue for miles and pointless detours. The natural home of the orange plastic cone. Normally we're diverted through Aberfeldy or something.

Now the DVLC has taken my license away, and without marvelous Slavey 17-year-old daughter's new licence, we'd be stuffed. She took us to the A9's fun-fest, the House of Bruar earlier today. A place to buy tartan, shortbread and Haggis. A place filled by people eager to vote 'yes' in September. A place to get out of.

Quite why Long-Suffering Wife and her family decided to spend their holidays all the way up here in the northwest of Scotland rather baffles me. It could hardly be further: when we cross the border, we are NOT YET HALFWAY!

It's flipping miles; but worth it, I guess. The scenery is fab, and there are some great hills to walk, super – if icy cold – swimming, if you like, or can manage, that sort of thing. It never hugely appealed to me, even when I could.

But the family have infected me with the Assynt bug too, so it's actually at my request that we are filling up at Inverness Tesco, only 2 hours to go to that freezing water.

Swimming, they say, is like riding a bike; once learned, never forgot. Cobblers. I can't ride a bike anymore either. I used to be quite a good swimmer; whereas formerly I swam like a fish, now I swim like a stone.

Round the last corner and there it is! Inverkirkaig. And the sun is out here while England is underwater. Ha!

13 Guinea pig
Wednesday 19 February

"It's not the despair. I can take the despair. It's the hope I can't stand." I know how John Cleese feels in that fairly crap, but good-in-parts movie, *Clockwise*.

For many years now, I have – reluctantly, slowly – been forced to address the inevitability that this progression has only one possible ending. At some point in the next few months or years, I will die, and that's that. It's taken a while – Long-Suffering Wife thinks I went totally round the bend for a while – but I think that I have finally got my head round it. And while I don't welcome it – I don't have a death wish, whatever L-SW may assert – I do accept its inevitability. Qué será será.

Now, the game has changed in a good – but disconcerting – way. And I'm a bit thrown, I must confess.

A good friend, E, is some sort of medical/scientific entrepreneur. Last week he came to me with a suggestion. Some stem cell people he's dealing with will be scouting for human guinea-pigs to try out their new procedure. Why don't I become one? It involves flying abroad and having some of my cells removed, fiddled with and reintroduced. And then, who knows?

Cure. It's not a concept I have even considered in the past years. For good reason. Thinking about it is a total (apols for bad language) mind-fuck. With despair, I knew where I stood. With hope, I'm rather at sea. I'm rather disappointed at myself for wanting it so much. Am I THAT shallow? There's something admirable about despair; something demeaning and pathetic about hope. For years, kind friends have been urging me not to abandon hope; but I did. It's easier that way. Now what? Maybe L-SW has been right all along, berating me for indolence at physio, trying to encourage my leg muscles not to fester. Or smoking. Will I have to look after myself now? Hell!

And now it's a wait. Will the stem cell people take me? When can I start? What counts as success? Walking again? Talking intelligibly? Using a pen? Remembering birthdays? Will it come back, even if it goes away? Will it still be ME if any of that happens? Cripes!

14
Sunday 23 February

Back down the A9 yesterday, with Slavey 17-year-old daughter taking all of that horrible Brigadoon road from Inverness to Perth, because Long-Suffering Wife can't be trusted.

Too fast or too slow? I don't mean the driving this time. The day before, to avoid the howling Scottish wind, we settled down for a video: *Ordinary People* is what passes for entertainment with us nowadays. But it set me athinking. The movie begins after the shocking and surprising death of the elder teenage son of Donald Sutherland and Mary Tyler Moore in a yachting accident: a death they can't come to terms with.

Those two words, shocking and surprising, by the way, are very different. It is quite possible for a death to be one and not the other: David Frost's passing last year was, certainly to me, who'd worked with him for over seven years, totally shocking and entirely unsurprising. I'd been expecting his demise for years.

A sudden and unexpected death can be both, but a descent like mine will surely be a shock – but can be no surprise to anyone who knows me.

Anyway am I going too fast, too slow – or neither? Actually, I think BOTH might be the right answer. Too fast? There are some things as yet undone, I'm not ready for it and I so want to know how things will turn out, for Long-Suffering Wife, for the kids, for lots of people.

Too slow? This exacerbation is pretty intolerable. I dribble, I slur my words, I'm incontinent, I fall over all the time. Every day it's hard to imagine that this could possibly get any worse – and every day it bleeding does; I discover something – usually a fairly trivial thing – which I did yesterday for the very last time without realising it, and the sense of loss, of grief, is ghastly.

Too fast AND too slow. The A9 writ large.

15
Wednesday 26 February

It sounds so easy. A special carriage on every train for wheelchairs. A guard gets a ramp to put you on the train, and they call ahead to your destination so that there's one waiting to get you off again. Perfect.

That's the theory, anyway. And it is great, when it works. But what if it doesn't? A few weeks ago, the train was delayed and there was nobody here at Cambridge to help me get the wheelchair off. The doors closed again, and the train zoomed off to Ely. Long-Suffering Wife had to phone the railway company who sent some apologetic flunkey to meet me at Ely. And stay with me back to Cambridge. Never again, I vowed.

So this week, when the train was delayed by half an hour into Cambridge, I was ready. But not ready enough, it transpired. Because the train was late, we were ushered to platform 7 here, and that meant I needed to manoeuvre out backwards.

I am a poor driver of this buggy. Even forwards, I crash all the time. I've had it less than a year, and it already looks more battered than the bus in The Italian Job. Backwards I'm even worse.

So I tried to creep slowly to the door to alert a guard to my presence. Honestly, I did. But it's hard to control, backwards. I shot out of the train, out of the chair, and the buggy ended upside down on top of me.

Actually it didn't hurt too much. My pride was more wounded than my body. But still. Looking forward even more to that stem cell trial now.

16
Saturday 1 March

Long-Suffering Wife put on one of her cabarets this week. Her temper, always spooky at the best of times, flies into the stratosphere when a cabaret is imminent (every couple of months). It's like PMT with knobs on: avoid.

Anyway, after the wonderful event, I had a natter with L-SW's friend, D. D is a neuroscientist, close to the absolute guru of MS, our very own Wizard of Oz, The Great Compston (TGC). Through TGC, D is checking out my imminent stem cell gubbins. (Please forgive all these bloody acronyms and capital letters).

But what do I want her or him to find out? If the conclusion is of the 'never heard of the guy – don't touch with a bargepole' kind, how will I feel?

This is – quite probably – my last roll of the dice. I've had it with this kind of existence. Why not give this stem cell thing a try? It's not like I have much choice.

On the other hand, is there a different set of dice I should be rolling? Should I waste my final days trawling the internet to become some kind of expert on whacky peer-reviews in obscure magazines?

And then there's the new fear: outcome. What will the doctors think of as a success? That I can speak without dribbling? That I can wipe my bum with my dominant left hand again? That they extend my life by two months?

Call that a success? Piss off! For me, it's cure or nothing. A Nobel Prize for the doc is no use to me, unless I'm free of this thing. And I don't want it coming back, neither.

17
Sunday 2 March

This piece will offend some of you. I apologise in advance. I am not deliberately offensive – it just happens that way.

It is often thought that, when you are in your last months, religion is a comfort. I believe the opposite. A friend, P, is a vicar who has visited and studied some 50 religious outfits, from the Vatican to Zoroastrian sky burials to obscure Cargo Cults in the South Pacific which venerate Prince Philip. But P found one common feature linking them all: belief in life after death. Whether by reincarnation or by purgatory, paradise or hell, religious folk of every stripe insist that The End is not the end. A simple test, therefore. If you believe in a hereafter, you're religious. If not, not.

Not me. But I'm not Dawkinsily smug about all this. Atheism is not a religion for me. There is plenty of tosh from both sides. And if you choose to believe in balderdash, that's your business. The point I want to make is different. It's that all those boring chilly hours in church, mosque or synagogue spent queuing for your wafer and sip or whatever AREN'T WORTH IT. You'll still be plagued with doubt, still be tormented in your final days. You wouldn't be human otherwise. This week, I'll be joining the audience in Westminster Abbey for a memorial service for a Methodist. I will even mutter my way through the prayers of thanks for the life of David Frost. But if I thought I'd ever meet him again on the 'other side', I'd kill myself. Not that it'll make any difference. Eternity with Frost? No thanks.

18
Monday 3 March

L-SW is on holiday for a week with her kind friend B. Off the grid, so I can't pester by email or text, as I usually do. She can recharge her batteries – which she will surely need for what is to come.

It's not something I know anything about, and it won't affect me, but I think about it all the time, even though it's none of my business. Like winning zillions on the Euromillions. Grief, bereavement. They aren't emotions that will affect me, I hope. But they are in store, probably, for those I love. Long-Suffering Wife will suffer more; and the kids. Crap.

At university, all those years ago, my flat-mate and friend, S, had us all reading CS Lewis' great book 'A Grief Observed', about his reaction to the loss of his beloved wife. A bit Christian for me, but hey ho. (Quite why S wanted us all to read her religious claptrap, I'll never know. Bristol was fruity then.)

The point is, was, that this thing came at him from unexpected angles, that it altered his perception of everyone else, making them seem feeble, chicken, if they talked about anything else than his loss; trivial if they did. A no-win situation; like the Euromillions.

I don't want that to happen to L-SW, or the kids, or my parents. But in a perverse and selfish way, I do. Not to be missed would be an insult, wouldn't it? But I will be. And, obviously, I won't be there to advise. Not that my advice is worth much, anyway. Particularly on that. Not by text, not by email.

19
Wednesday 5 March

My parents, with whom I'm staying, gave me a hard time at lunchtime in the pub today. They've been copied in on these pieces, and they don't much care for the relentlessly negative tone.

It's true. The pieces are gloomy. I'm sorry about that. So this week, I've decided to be more upbeat. Sunny. Cheerful. You won't get me totally changing my tune. I'm still dying, it will still be soonish and it's hard to be too positive about that, but this piece is supposed to mark a change; so, let's go.

Next Tuesday is a biggie. This stem cell malarkey may then become clearer. Long-Suffering Wife and I will be trekking off to London for a meeting with E and his Danish colleagues about it all. Isn't Denmark lovely? The Bridge. Bacon. Butter. In particular, I want to pin down a timescale, so that the medics can't pull out, and so it happens before I take any turns for the worse.

The lovely physio, Elliott, came today to give me some exercises. He is trying to ensure that my muscles are working should they be needed after the stem cell procedure. His white coat was smart; so was his watch.
Right. That's enough positivity. Bollocks to that.

20
Thursday 6 March

Fifteen-year-old Too-Cool-For-School middle daughter has been sent off at 6.45am on a Spanish exchange trip to Barcelona. She went off, predictably, without her iPhone, which she's lost, thus forcing me to open a Facebook account in our dog's name (don't ask!) to maintain contact.

Barcelona has a bad association with dogs for me. The last time we went there, our beloved pug drowned in a swimming pool while we were away. Now, I'm not comparing myself to a pug – though many would – but it's the only comparison I have. So, is the death of a person – husband, father or friend – a bit like losing a pug, just worse?

There's no doubt that it was bad when Emily died. We all loved her, a lot. We missed her, we cried, we ordered brandy. But, and here's the nub, we got over it. And, in time, people will get over me. There's no cause for guilt or shame in that. It's what happens. It's good.

21
Tuesday 11 March

Number 21, or in Pontoon, vingt-et-un. An ace and a ten. Let's hope so, anyway.

The meeting happened, and it looks definite that I will be a stem cell guinea pig later in the year. A bit more of a wait than I'd hoped for – maybe not till August – but hey. Don't run before you can walk, they say. And I certainly can't walk. For now, anyway.

The Shard restaurant wasn't open, so we assembled in a Borough Market cafe where E and the doctor, C, ate freebie but small curries while we chatted about neural stem cell whatsits, and whether we could accelerate things by going to Quebec, or Moscow, or Copenhagen. The doctor was impressively no-nonsense, convincing Long-Suffering Wife in a way that no number of us hopeless males can do. The secretive cloak-n-dagger nature of the meeting was a bit spooky, but hey ho. Thankfully, she batted away L-SW's suggestion that I might need to get fit before treatment. Now Dr C only needs to rope in help from my lovely MS nurse, Mary, and spookily erudite neurologist, The Great Compston, and we're away. Hopefully.

Dr C and E eating tiny curries in Borough Market.

22
Wednesday 12 March

I should just say that the following has little or nothing to do with my 2 favourite subjects:
1. Me, or
2. Dying.
Apologies in advance to the disappointed. Normal service will be resumed shortly. Instead I'm going to talk about a rigorously scientific experiment and a man who died this morning.

Some years ago I used to produce a chat show. I invited three guests, all of whom have been described as 'the nicest man in the world', Michael Palin, King Constantine of Greece, and Tony Benn. So the challenge was obvious. Who was the nicest nicest man? My Slavey daughter, then thirteen, and her best friend, Elodie, kindly came along to the green room where all three were sitting to chat. Slavey was primed to 'fall 'over. Elodie asked to spill her drink. So, who was the kindest to girls in distress? The green room door was closed, the girls left alone with their unsuspecting 'subjects'. The results are in. It's so close etc, etc. Michael Palin, very nice, but talked about himself too much. King Constantine, also very nice. Emanated regality, ditto his son. 'You could tell he was a Prince', apparently, with his red silk hankie so neat in his breast pocket. But the clear winner from both judges was Wedgie. He talked to the girls, listened, made valid points. Officially the nicest nicest man in the world.

One other thing I must say. In my last post I misrepresented and upset my Long-Suffering Wife, who did not, repeat NOT, find the cloak-n-dagger aspect of our Tuesday stem cell meeting fun or attractive. She hated it, I'm told, sternly

Thursday 13 March

Helter-skelter week. The stem cell meeting on Tuesday, funeral on Wednesday, memorial on Thursday.

The memorial was for David Frost, and was in Westminster Abbey, because a stone with his name was laid, incongruously, alongside Tennyson and Wordsworth.

Because the Abbey had to put ramps down to get my buggy in, we were just about the last ones in the nave. Someone assumed we must, therefore, have been royals, so the 2000 massed celebs stood up and bowed as we entered.

Actually, the service was pretty good. Fond address by Greg Dyke, funny poem from Joanna Lumley. David would have loved it.

The celebs didn't make the same mistake on the way out and there was a scrum to make it into daylight. I ran over Anne Widdecombe's toes. But she deserved it – she once got me and Janet Street Porter banned from Glasgow by the city council, after I wrote a hugely witty script about shackled women and baseball bats (long story).

Less good news on the stem cell front. The Great Compston [Prof Alastair Compston] has declined to meet with my proto-medics. So maybe it's off. Probably it was just a pipe dream anyway. But comforting while it lasted.

My good friend R has invited me to Thailand for 3 weeks, starting Wednesday. I shall learn to meditate and be calm. Ommm. My body is a temple etc.

24
Tuesday 18 March

Living, as we now do, in Swotsville, the Cambridge Science Festival is this week's highlight. On Saturday I took Climb-anything 13-year-old son to an exhibition about eyes – and he enjoyed it, promise.

Then on Monday, Long-Suffering Wife took me to a lecture on stem cells and MS. It was interesting, exciting even – until L-SW made the schoolboy error of asking a question without already knowing the answer.

"How long can damaged cells survive without intervention? Years?"
"No, weeks. Months at most."
Bugger.

E, the friend who has got me even partially involved with stem cell guinea piggery, warns me not to lose hope.

But it's simpler. Now I'm on a plane, heading for Thailand. Watching a pants movie where Sly Stallone escapes from a CIA uber-high security prison hulk, helped by a bearded Arnie. Combined age, approx 130. Escape from a paper bag is more plausible for these codgers. Shawshank it ain't. Why do I always choose the straight-to-video crappest films on a flight? I'm craning my neck out of the window in the forlorn hope that I spot that missing 777 Flight* in some backwoods airport and thus win Nobel Prize etc.

As if they are the only family I know, E's brother-in-law, R, will be my host in Bangkok. He has organised a few days for me to learn relaxation and meditation. Good luck with that one, I reckon. Arguably the most distressing things out here may be the warm and the water. I wilt in hot weather - and, perhaps most creepily, I can't swim anymore. So I'll probably be indoors most of the time. Indoors and not upstairs, cos I can't do them anymore either. I'll be entirely reliant on my buggy, too. So here's hoping that I find a way to recharge it. My bag was packed by Too-Cool-for-School 15-year-old daughter, who may have left charger out on purpose

*Malaysian Airlines Flight 370, which disappeared on March 8 2014, shortly after departing from Kuala Lumpur for Beijing

Friday 21 March

In a way, I guess it makes me an easy guest. All I do out here is sleep. And kip. And doze. It's not jetlag, I think, I got onto Thai time straightaway. I know what time it is at home – about 11am. My iPad clock hasn't been changed. But it's suppertime here, and feels it. I am just a lazy arse, I suppose, and go to bed a lot. About four times a day, only surfacing for a meal or a fag or both. Perfect.

Sleep. It's important, they say. That's my excuse, anyway. My sleep is fitful. Always has been. I don't dream, for example, or haven't for yonks. I don't think I ever have: When people recount their nighttime adventures to me in long detail, I am tempted to think that: They are liars, and/or they are bores.

(Thinking that people who are different from me are bullshitting is a natural state. When people tell me of their love for dark beer, hatred of marmite or attachment to 16th century poetry and the art of Rothko, I will nod sagely in agreement. Meanwhile I am thinking 'what a whopper; piss off, pretentious dullard.')

Sleep for me is a very two-edged sword. It revives, yes. But not as much as those self-help books suggest, and there's an inevitable concern that it's a waste of time. There's two hours I won't get back. So sleeping is both welcome and at the same time fearful. Like Marmite.

Off south tomorrow, when the real meditation begins.

26
Tuesday 25 March

Calm, Calm, Calm, clear, and some other word that begins with C, which I forget. All is calm. All is that C word (no, not that one!)

I have come out to Phuket for meditation. My teacher, Anamai, is a former Buddhist monk. He now specialises in passing on his Wisdom to arses like me. This place is lovely, serene, and all thanks to the generosity of kind friend R.

Still no date, or even country, confirmed for this Stem Cell malarkey. Oh my God! No, breathe. Deep. All is well. If it happens, happy. If not, happy too. Loving kindness.

I am calm. No, that's not right. Anamai says that there is no I. I, me, the self. I am not calm: there is calmness. It's bloody hot here. I haven't dared go out in the sun at all. My eyesight is a goner anyway.

Not sleeping too well here. I blame the heat. Or I would if I were the sort of unenlightened person who blamed anything. Got Radio 4 on this iPad, so can listen all night to Moral Maze at 3.00am, World Tonight at 5, Today programme at lunch (gazpacho), WatO [Radio 4's The World at One] with supper. GMT+7.

Death is just a change; everything changes. No need for fear, or obsession. if I die, I die. It's no biggie. Death may be coming, but that's for the future. And the future is not a concern. Nor are those who will be left behind. What matters is the Here and Now. Planning is pointless and damaging.

Swimming first, and I really have made progress there. My swimming physio, Naomi, is from Barcelona. Lovely, pretty, kind, nose like a Shand*. I did a width yesterday. Doesn't sound like much, but it was amazing, believe me. I never thought I would ever swim again. Thanks, R, despite your passion for green tea, which looks like bat piss and tastes worse.

This hotel is built on steep slopes, too vertical for my buggy, so poor R has to push me all the time. Good for him, I persuade myself, calmly calm. Lots of people, notably D and B and Long-Suffering Wife, have justifiably complained about how angry some of these pieces are.

No more; goodbye anger, hello calmness.

*Dear friends with big noses

27 Spam
Friday 28 March

Are you baffled to be getting this? Blame google. By default, my gmail sends to pretty much everyone I've ever written to, and that means YOU. Hard cheese. That doesn't mean you have to READ it. Get a better spam filter.

A related concern: how long after they have died should you delete someone from your contacts? This piece will probably go to the email account of David Frost. Maybe even Vincent Hanna*. I don't suppose they'll even need that spam filter.

But wouldn't it be a bit sick to be expunging them, just because they happen to be dead? Isn't that blatantly deadist? And isn't deadism one of the worst isms?

Long-Suffering Wife has been working with builders, Occupational Therapists, planners, grants officers, and architects, using spreadsheets and charm. While I am swanning around in Thailand (flotation tank tomorrow), she is trying to keep the show on the road. Not easy when I haven't earned a bean in 2014 and nobody wants to employ a misanthropic cripple who may well pop it.

If – and I emphasise if – we do get a grant, then phase 2 building begins, lasts till end June, and you are all invited to a knees-up in Cambridge. Whoever you are.

*A presenter on Channel 4's *A Week in Politics*

28 Hua Hin, Thailand
Friday 4 April

It's early morning here; a good time to be up cos the temperature is very tolerable. In a few hours, I'll have to be indoors. Leave the midday sun to the mad dogs.

The relationship between MS and heat is weird. Get born in a hot place, and you probably won't get it. Even quite small temperature differences seem to be massively important. You're much likelier to get MS if you grow up in Scotland than England, Canada than the US.

But if you have it, then avoid hot countries. I get a lot worse in the sun. First my eyesight gets even less dependable. Blurred and double. Then the bleeding tremor starts. My leg jumps about in a way which might be funny – if it were happening to anyone else. I feel exhausted, can hardly keep my eyes open.

Actually, falling asleep at the wrong time is one of the first symptoms. I'm probably one of the only people alive who can truthfully say that I dozed off while Janet S-P was talking. Janet is scary enough to keep most people awake. Not me, and that was about the year 2000, during morning conference at the Sindie. I've been snoozing ever since.

But heat is now a bigger menace: I've been in seaside places for most of the past 3 weeks, but haven't yet dared go on a beach. Even at a London test match, in full sun for a day, I wilt and fall over. Falling over is quite funny for fans of Laurel and Hardy. I bet they didn't laugh either.

Neither Lords not the Oval are any good for wheelchairs anyway. The concrete bleachers are hard to get to, particularly when you're trying to carry a healthy balanced diet of twiglets (vegetable), Quavers (carbohydrate) Porky Scratchings (protein) AND cider (fruit) at the same time. With that lot in me, not even Jimmy Anderson's bowling will keep me awake.

29 The plane back
Wednesday 9 April

My buggy weighs a ton. Well, not exactly; but the battery on its own is 35kilos and the chair without battery is about the same. I have to know this sort of garbage because airlines ask it at check-in. Then some surly man in one of those ugly jackets will make me sign 3 forms (with trembling hand) tag the buggy, remove the battery and then put it on the plane. To Reykjavik, probably.

Which leaves me. Some other be-jacketed guy will then plonk me in his corporate chair, wheel me through the bowels of the airport, down in eerie lifts, through a door marked BEWARE OF THE LEOPARD, past baggage reclaim, queue barging my way through passport control and then – without explanation – piss off for a fag or something, never to be seen again. It's up to me to handle the chair to the plane door – a hell of a shag, even with my new-found Buddhist calmness. I'll then be transferred onto ANOTHER narrower chair, and up the aisle backwards to my seat.

So that's where I am now. 42H. Over Kabul, according to the moving map. Moving maps, by the way, are just about the coolest invention of our age. And what a groovy job to be the person who decides which towns to highlight. What a good use for that Geography PhD, Tamara! Who would otherwise know that Belarus had a Pinsk as well as Minsk, or that Borisov is the only other noteworthy Belorussian town, and is not just the proposed new name for London.

There's a huge mental difference between seemingly endless queueing and just waiting. For most air travellers, the zigzag queues - for passport control, immigration, boarding, carousel etc etc – are the worst of air travel. So frustrating. For us in wheelchairs, there are never queues – we get wheeled straight to the front every time. The buggy's in Oversized Baggage. No queue – no people at all, in fact.

But the price is paid in the waiting. Many hours today just parked in an airport wheelchair, unable to go anywhere. Its mind-numbingly boring instead of toe-curlingly frustrating. Like this tedious *Hunger Games* movie I'm watching.

Finally, I must apologise that this is bigger and more bandwidth-consuming than usual. Friends, sceptical of my new enlightenment, wanted photographic proof of my Thai trip. So here it is; yesterday 6am (yes, early rising is a part of new Zen me.)

Lunch with Sue* on Friday, so maybe this stuff will go online again and spare you this email rubbish. And sorting the stem cell gubbins with E, so expect news soon. But I am calm calm calm either way.

---

*Sue Douglas launched the digital version of *people.co.uk* where 'Dying for Beginners' first appeared as a column in November 2013

30 Roy Castle
Thursday 17 April

In answer to your many queries, no date, or even location yet, for the Stem Cell doo-dah. Not Canada, for sure. I would have had to prove long term residency in Canada to qualify for that one, and not even my impressive collection of Douglas Coupland novels and Joni Mitchell albums was sufficient to convince them of my inner Mountie.

A couple of doc-makers want to make a film about the procedure, and I had a couple of hours with them at BAFTA in Piccadilly this week, which was very nice. I even had my coffee paid for. But I couldn't tell them much, because I simply don't know. When the guy in the know comes over next month, perhaps more will be clear. At the moment, I'm as ignorant as you.

So, symptoms. Only a few years ago or so, when I first got it, this tremor was really FUNNY. It's hard to remember now, but it was. I even filmed it then cos it was such a riot – hand shaking and no stopping it. Climb-anything son had us all in stitches with his impersonation. Now it's got into my legs too. and is nothing but a pest. Long -Suffering Wife has to endure permanent toe tapping on my buggy. More taps, faster and noisier, than Roy Castle. But there was a time, and if I could only recapture that....

Charlie in Hua Hin, Thailand

40

31 Liars
Sunday 20 April

It is amazing, impressive. Lying comes naturally to some people, particularly politicians, of course. But there are some – and I've only met a couple – Bashir of Sudan and Aliyev of Azerbaijan spring to mind – who make you gasp and stretch your eyes at their brazenness. Total unashamed whoppers, and they know that you know that they know that you know etc.

I guess its a part of my Huguenot heritage; I hate lying almost more than anything. Swearing is fine, quite funny, even. But lying offends me hugely.

But – and here's the rub – where does one draw the line between lying and not being totally frank? Is it incumbent on me to bang on about what I can't do all the time, or do I leave it to others to find it out? One example. The last time I went anywhere without this chair was the last job interview I had, at BBC White City. I did take sticks, and did fall a lot, but I made it. I reasoned that if they needed to know about my health, they'd ask. But I did feel bad. All academic anyway. I didn't get the job. President Aliyev did, probably.

Happy Easter.

32 Honesty
Friday 25 April

It's cabaret week in Cambridge again, so Long-Suffering Wife is in a fraught mood. Plus the builders are getting phase 2 underway, which means I have to decamp to Essex again, for the best part of 2 months this time.

I have written before, last week in fact, about my dislike of lying. But there's a flipside, and perhaps I err too much on the wrong side of it: brutal honesty. I emphasise the 'brutal' bit – cos frankly I'm an arse. Ask anyone.

It's sometimes quite a hoot to be frank, but not necessarily a good idea. I quit one job of supposedly funny stuff at the Beeb some years ago and sent an honest assessment to the guy in charge, P. 'Can the BBC do satire?' I wondered. 'Not with this bunch of incompetents' I concluded. I expected thanks, but P threatened to sue me if I ever wrote of my experience. Does this count? Or the time I wrote an honest review of a news/entertainment programme, and said it was 'quite simply the worst programme anywhere, ever, in the history of time. You have got to see this…' My friend M concluded that I'd never again get a job at the Beeb. He was right.

This honesty obsession has a big downside: the kids. It's obvious to them that I'm worsening. But is it fair of me to answer questions about my future truthfully? Its only a couple of years since Climb-anything Son believed in fairies and Father Christmas. Is he ready to face death? No, is the answer. Honestly.

33 Shrink rapt
Tuesday 29 April

Another Addenbrooke's appointment, with a psychiatrist this time. Although in a drear corridor, the room is supposed to be matey. A bit like the TV room, except no TV. Green carpet, comfy chairs, plenty of space.

This is the third Addenbrooke's shrink I've seen, and none of them have fitted the Hollywood stereotype. Not male, not sixty-something, not beardies. Perhaps Jewish, but I never asked.

The problem with seeing someone new every time is that it takes an hour every time to answer the same old questions. Yes, I am on Prozac. No, no allergies.

The psychiatrist was nice, friendly, didn't fall asleep. She'll write to my GP. Maybe I'll see her again, maybe not, and I can answer those same questions again to someone else.

The real trouble with today's Cameroonie NHS seems not to be a lack of staff – it's more a falling-between-stools thing. Everyone knows what MS is; even me. But not being a quick-fix thing makes it a nuisance.

I haven't seen a consultant since 2012. A relief, really. They have little to offer. The real hero – or heroine – of my MS life is the wonderful M, my MS nurse. M I see often, today even. Despite the construction chaos, she even visited my home. We talked of builders, of kids, of that spooky sound I make in my throat, which not even I can tell is laughter or tears, when neither is appropriate anyway.

Anyway, kids. Must go to bed. It's Long Suffering Wife's birthday tomorrow, heralding my favourite 6 weeks of the year, during which she is a whole year older than me. But we will probably be woken early by wakeful kids demanding thanks for presents which I bought anyway. Goodnight.

34 Totally Spastic
Thursday 1 May

I'm sitting in bed. It's 7.30am and I want to go for a piss. My buggy is only a foot away. Simples, eh?

No. I can't flipping move, not even an inch. If I try to get into the chair, I'll end up on the floor. But if I don't, I'll wet myself. Hmmm. A two pipe problem, except I don't smoke in bed. Nor am I quite cheesy enough to do pipes, Sherlock.

Before he became pornographer-in-chief, Nicholson Baker wrote some very good detailed novels about small amounts of time. Like a lunch-break or bottle-feeding a baby. This transfer, bed to buggy, is tailor made for such a book.

My hands, arms, are fine. It's my legs I can't move at all. Yelling for help pretty pointless. Admirable though her qualities are, Long-Suffering Wife is pretty miniscule, not very strong and I've had too much of her yummy birthday carrot cake yesterday and am too big to carry.

My Buddhist guru, A, says I should live in the present, the Here and Now. All very well, but right here, right now, i need a pee. And I just got an email from E, delaying the stem cell visit, so I'm gonna have to delay the camera crew*. Chiz.

Spasticity is odd. I absolutely know what I want to do, and probably how. It's really easy. I just need to grab this sheet and tug till I move. But the sheet keeps slipping through fingers. Damn. Think again. Calm calm. But I still need a pee!

It's also quite interesting, being spastic. And it's a meaningful word. If lesbians call themselves dykes, and blacks reclaim Niggas, then isn't it time that we took the term spastic back from the likes of Alan Clark – who used it as a term of abuse?

Bollocks! Got to the buggy and my leg is caught underneath. Pull it, swing it manually, then go, go, go.

*A friend of Sue Douglas started to make a documentary about Charlie's stem cell treatment

35 Heavy Petting
Thursday 8 May

Disabled loos and changing rooms have a bit of reddy-orange string which connects to the ceiling, and thence to a rather noisy alarm. So you MUST NOT pull the cord if you have sneaked into the loo for
a) bit of queue barging or
b) Some illicit nookie with new girlfriend.
Or you'll get caught and have to fake a limp, which convinces nobody.
But now there's a new problem. Don't use the cord for what it's meant, either.

Last week, in my post-Thai fitness zealotry, I went to the swimming pool for disabled swimming. The actual dip was ok, despite the pool being a bit overrun with supertanned carers practising their backstrokes and ignoring the 'No running, No diving, No bombing, No Heavy Petting' signs - while their charges floundered in the deep end. Anyway, on exiting the pool, I went into the disabled changing room. I removed my trunks – and fell over. I tried to get up – and fell over.

No problem. From my floor position, I reached for the red cord. And pulled. A satisfying alarm sounded. Footfalls outside. But no offer of help or 'are you OK in there?' query. Instead, the alarm was simply switched off. And the footfalls went away again. 'Help. Help' I yelled. But it was too late.

I did, eventually, manage to clamber back into my buggy. But it hurt like crazy and took ages.

This morning, Dave, snapper for the local paper, took some pictures of me to accompany the story. (Have you noticed that snappers are usually called Dave, whereas TV camera guys on live OBs are all Phil? It's the other way round in South Africa: a telling, but uninteresting statistic). Nearly a week after the event, I don't think I looked upset enough for Dave.

36 Memory
Saturday 10 May

I expect that I've written about this before, but I don't remember. And that's the point. Always a bit rubbish, my memory has pretty much completely gone. So have I gone too? Or have I at least changed beyond recognition?

One example. About twenty-something years ago, before we were married, Long-Suffering Wife and I took a break. I went out with another girl, R. It ended, although we loved each other very much. I think it was my fault. BUT I DON'T REMEMBER. If it sounds callous, it probably is. But it's also true. I don't remember, anything. I remember R's white towelling dressing-gown, and that's about it.

I know that I used to remember, but no longer can. God, I'm a shit. The time was when I could name every one of the 650 MPs and their constituency. In those days I read Hansard every day, and was in the lobby. Now I'm not – foreign rather than domestic affairs have been my thing for years now – and I can no longer name more than a handful of constituencies. That no longer matters – doesn't everyone forget stuff as we age? But it matters to me.

So who am I? Others seem to recognise me as the person I was, but I increasingly don't recognise them.
"Hi Charlie. How are you?"
"Fine"'. Who the hell are you? But I don't say that. It might offend.

I'm back to Essex imminently while walls are bashed down in Cambridge and Too-cool-for-school 15-year-old daughter entertains her Spanish exchange. (Whose name is something like 'Nerys'* but can't be. Welsh, not Spanish). On Monday I'm having lunch with S to discuss her internet plans. Then the stem cell guy comes over here on the following week, and I'll meet with him so I'll keep you informed about progress.

If I remember.

*It was 'Neus'

R, circa 1992

37 Underworldonomics
Tuesday 13 May

L unch with S on Monday. She's making progress, I think. Then it's stem cell stuff next week.

Meal with S was at swanky Langan's. But I can't do that again. Its too humiliating. My spasticated legs went into a crap spasm, and the poor Langan's waiter – who'd already had to retrieve my fish pie mess – had to try to cram my unhelpful body back into my buggy. And my voice had gone.

S is cutting deals with people all around, which might give her/me, access to hacks in odd places. Which has revived, for me, a suggestion I made to Al Jazeera a year ago and it went nowhere – the price I pay for being seen as rather insane and overly excitable. If any of you can run with it, please do. I'm not up to it anymore.

For the benefit of those of you who aren't in telly, and are in some dimwit medium instead (papers, radio etc), I'll speak slowly. Take, say, 4 random but far-apart cities (eg Athens, Rio, Jo'burg, Tokyo) where you have access to lazy-but-desperate hacks with nothing better to do who can speak with underworld contacts.
Then, for each city, get a price for each of:
A kidnap
A gram of cocaine
Half an hour with a prostitute

Then collate and compare.
Jazeera weren't brave enough. You be. Wow, cool. I'd watch.

38
Wednesday 14 May

No stem cell meet this week. E is at Stem Cell Catapult conference in Bishopsgate. The meeting will be next week now. And the camera crew should be there. And I have a putative timetable. I should be injected next November.

That's the good news.

But I have to organise the 'harvesting' of some of my bone marrow and get it shipped to Canada by September. And I haven't a clue how to go about it. It isn't, as my neurologist friend G observes, like harvesting courgettes. It needs a haematologist, probably a private clinic, a cheque book – and it hurts.

I don't have a neurologist, and my GP has just retired. If anyone out there has any tips, I'd be ever so.

Back to Essex tomorrow, to avoid builders, then back here for a consultation with SALT [Speech and Language Therapy] team, who might help me speak or swallow better. It's dull for everyone, but necessary.

Long-Suffering Wife has been urging me to write some memoirs for my kids to read – ahem – after. So spent the day doing that. Much of what I wrote she will have her own – very different – recollection of.

But using the tried and tested journalist's formula – first simplify, then exaggerate – this is my version.

39 Salt
Thursday 22 May

Speech And Language Therapy, they call it, which makes for a groovy acronym – better for sure than Swallowing Or Dribbling, which it might as easily be.

This week I had a home visit from Leanne of the SALT team, who passed on some tips on how to avoid choking (chin to chest and swallow), and how to speak more clearly and understandably – cos people keep hanging up on me (talk slow, think loud).

Leanne gave me some white powder which I should mix into drinks (water, coffee, not wine, we didn't discuss Bloody Mary) to make them thicker and more drinkable. She even brought along an amplifier gizmo which, if it becomes necessary, would make my voice's volume better. Modern tech is amazing.

But surely there's a limit. With the physio, Elliot, I spend most of my time thinking of cunning plans to do everyday tasks like hold a phone or cross my legs. But MS is a wanker. It probably means that I won't die in tremendous pain. But the fairly manageable death comes with a pretty horrid life, and there comes a point…

But not yet. I still have a last roll of the dice; this Stem Cell gubbins. A kind godmother has been researching haematologists who might be able to do the bone marrow harvesting I'll need. On we go….

40 Maps
Saturday 24 May

It sounds so simple. The person in the driver's seat drives, the passenger navigates. But it's scary.

Too-cool-for-school 15-year-old daughter has gone for an outward bound camp trip which will count towards her Duke of Edinburgh bronze award. She may at least learn to read a map. More than I can do.

It is hugely tempting to ascribe all of my uselessnesses to this disease. Can't read a map? Must be MS fault. But it isn't. I was never any good with maps. My parents swear by the GPS they have in the car. My wife just swears.

The fact is that the Gods Eye View from above of a map baffles me. Ironically, I love maps. I once wrote a programme script for my friend JSP, in which she walked from Edinburgh to London in a straight line. We needed very detailed maps to plan her route. I still have them. But I never look at them. They scare me.

Ordnance Survey have this week announced that they will no longer be making the old-style 2d pathfinder maps we are used to. Apparently, with Google Maps available, demand has dropped off (wrong turn at Beachy Head or something). My daughter will know the way!

Stem Cell meeting this Friday. Apparently E, my medical friend, may have a solution for the 'harvesting' problem. A race against time now, cos I seem to be worsening by the day. A map, someone, fast.

41 The meet

Friday 30 May

Came down on the train to Kings Cross. Met off the platform by camera crew of 3, G [the director] and a couple of assistants, who filmed me buggying through the crowds and lighting a fag. That'll make for must-see TV! Took a cab all of the 100 yards to our UCH meeting place with E and J, the first of those stem cell wonks I have yet met.

It was a pretty good meet. Obviously, I was on an unfamiliar side of the camera, and the radio mic was a bit annoying – but hey. J was friendly, chatty. He had answers to our questions. Together with E, he is confident that the bone marrow harvesting can and will happen. He was expecting me to be considerably worse than I am – which I took as a compliment, of sorts. And he liked my Long-Suffering Wife, which was, therefore, reciprocated.

The meeting room had been chosen by the film crew and was hence all sterile white walls and electric sockets above the work surfaces, to look medical and sciency. As the first putative guinea pig for this treatment, everyone expected me to be bursting with concerns – will I turn into a gorilla etc. But I was happy to be putty in J's hands. After all, it's not like I've got masses of choice about where to invest my faith. J was fretting about how this thing might turn out in 5 or 10 years. Frankly, I'd be grateful for 5 or 10 months, symptom-free.

Afterwards we trooped off to St Pancras Old Church to hear a concert by my cousin Polly, ten years on from her first album launch. She was supported by old friends on double bass, mandolin and Hammond organ. It was a happy and life-affirming occasion. Let's hope the trial is similar.

Tuesday 3 June

Back in Essex to avoid builders who are making noise and mess in Cambridge. Desperately trying to read Lolita on Kindle ahead of book group meeting tomorrow. Reading this way means I can up the font size to legibility for a blind-as-a-bat reader like me. And you get to see other peoples' swotty marginalia notes. The downside is that with only about 4 lines per page, I have to spend most of my time flipping pages. And it makes even a short novella like this look intimidatingly ginormous with hundreds of pages etc.

One of the joys of being back here is that I was booked in to see my old groovy neurologist, G. He is of the Harold Shipman bow-tie wearing type. G is spectacularly unkeen on this Stem Cell stuff, but given my relative lack of choices, it's all wonderful to me, and G is humouring my keenness.

G has booked me in for an MRI scan in Braintree in a few weeks. He'll then write some guff based on that MRI, saying that I have indeed got progressive MS, and am therefore eligible for the trial. G also scored me on the Expanded Disability Status Scale with an 8.5 (where zero is normal, 10 is dead) – pretty bad, but any fool can see that.

Now, back to Lolita.

43 Carers
Sunday 8 June

I've got clean hair today. I had clean hair yesterday. And the day before etc. It's something for the Carers to do. I've never had such clean hair.

Every morning at around 730, a carer arrives at our house to shower, shampoo and dress me. It's rarely the same one, cos there are nearly 30 on the team. So I usually have to spend a while explaining that no, this is not a commune and yes, the coffee is in the jar with 'coffee' written on it etc.

With the house in such a shambles from builders, it's actually quite a help, taking some burden off Long-Suffering Wife, who gets a few more minutes to snooze before the kids are demanding a cooked breakfast. Then the carer has to turf me out of bed and plonk me in a wheelchair. My 'wet room' is right next to my bedroom and I do my first catheter of the day while the Carer warms up the shower. Then it's into the plastic showerproof wheelchair and under the jet for yet another hair wash. Out of the shower, get dry and then the Carer dries me. Having a stranger see me nude, or towel what they sweetly call my 'private area' is something you just have to get over. When your legs don't work and you can't really see properly, these things just happen.

Now clothes. If I've been sufficiently forward-thinking, I will have already laid out my outfit the night before. Pigs might fly. So we spend some time choosing things to wear. Because my wife's clothes are in the same room, I'm offered her black spangly size 5 shoes to put on. No thanks, those size 12 deck shoes, please. Showered, dressed, coffee in hand. I'm ready for another day. The carer fills in the yellow folder and goes, leaving the cleanest hair in Cambridge.

44 Timing
Tuesday 10 June

Perhaps the most irksome thing is the uncertainty. That I am on the way out is indubitable. More than 1, fewer than 5, remember. And that first 1 is pretty much done now, so let's call it more than zero, fewer than 4.

But when? And is there any way of knowing? Yesterday I really thought that it was uber-close. I couldn't see, and I kept falling out of my buggy. But today? I'm still here and on the train to Kings Cross for lunch with mates. Relief. But also quite annoying.

When hideous regimes – like the Yanks – want to dole out the ultimate penalty to murderers, etc. then they tell the felon just exactly when and how their end will come. March the 3rd, 9pm, lethal injection etc. It must be pretty horrible, that foreknowledge – counting the minutes down.

But how about not knowing the when or how? Just knowing it's soon. That's what MS is like. I'm now at 8.5 on that scale which goes to 10.

It's that harmless-looking "due to" in number 10 which is the most spooky. As I've said before, MS is not fatal. Few people die of MS. But plenty die due to it. Bollocks.

As an atheistic arse, I'm not afraid of dying. I'm far more afraid of making a twit of myself by assuming too much too early. I had a Dutch godfather who, given six months to live, spent all his money – and lived 10 years in misery and penury. Look again at that list. It's 9.5 that I really fear – inability to communicate. Give me 10 over 9.5 any day.

Here it is:

EXPANDED DISABILITY STATUS SCALE (EDSS) SCORE DESCRIPTION

1.0 No disability, minimal signs in one FS*

1.5 No disability, minimal signs in more than one FS

2.0 Minimal disability in one FS

2.5 Mild disability in one FS or minimal disability in two FS

3.0 Moderate disability in one FS, or mild disability in three or four FS. No impairment to walking

3.5 Moderate disability in one FS and more than minimal disability in several others. No impairment to walking

4.0 Significant disability but self-sufficient and up and about some 12 hours a day. Able to walk without aid or rest for 500m

4.5 Significant disability but up and about much of the day, able to work a full day, may otherwise have some limitation of full activity or require minimal assistance. Able to walk without aid or rest for 300m

5.0 Disability severe enough to impair full daily activities and ability to work a full day without special provisions. Able to walk without aid or rest for 200m

5.5 Disability severe enough to preclude full daily activities. Able to walk without aid or rest for 100m

6.0 Requires a walking aid – cane, crutch, etc – to walk about 100m with or without resting

6.5 Requires two walking aids – pair of canes, crutches, etc – to walk about 20m without resting

7.0 Unable to walk beyond approximately 5m even with aid. Essentially restricted to wheelchair; though wheels self in standard wheelchair and transfers alone. Up and about in wheelchair some 12 hours a day

7.5 Unable to take more than a few steps. Restricted to wheelchair and may need aid in transferring. Can wheel self but cannot carry on in standard wheelchair for a full day and may require a motorised wheelchair

8.0 Essentially restricted to bed or chair or pushed in wheelchair. May be out of bed itself much of the day. Retains many self-care functions. Generally has effective use of arms

8.5 Essentially restricted to bed much of day. Has some effective use of arms retains some self care functions

9.0 Confined to bed. Can still communicate and eat

9.5 Confined to bed and totally dependent. Unable to communicate effectively or eat/swallow

10.0 Death due to MS

*Functional Systems

45 Dates
Saturday 14 June

I was never any good at remembering dates, even when I had a decent memory, all of…ooh. last year or something. So it's always been a boon to me that we got married on my birthday. I have only to remember one date. It marks the end of that glorious annual joke-fest during which my Long-Suffering Wife (decrepit 48) is a year older than me (mere stripling 47). To celebrate our magnificent 20 years, we'll be off for the night in Suffolk. (Usually a punishment, admittedly; the journey from Cambridge to here in Essex is glorious, except for the 5 hideous minutes spent in ugly Suffolk, bypassing a town with a stupid metal logo*. The whole county is just a slab of concrete, anyway, for US aeroplanes. But Suffolk will be Springwatch-lovely this time, honest.)

The 18th of June. I guess it was chosen as the day for great battles – Waterloo and Orgreave – because its usually dry and warm. Because here's an interesting fact: it never rains on my birthday (remember the television footage of Orgreave – all sweaty, fat miners in t-shirts in blazing heat, with Scargill in a silly baseball cap). If you are planning a party etc for next year, remember the date: it doesn't rain on 18 June, and that's a guarantee. Unless it does.

Slavey Eldest daughter is also 18 this week, and has to do her final A Level on her birthday. Meanwhile, I now have a Stem Cell date from J, the scientist in charge. The 'harvesting' of my bone marrow will be in Sept, with the re-injections due to begin on December 1st. Happy Anniversary. So, by the time of my 49th, next June I'll either be cured or dead. Or neither.

*Haverhill

46 Red
Sunday 15 June

I was never a fan. Not football, you arse (although I don't much care for that either; not since J sacked me as goalie). I mean Wittgenstein of course (avoid). Doing him in philosophy was something of a chore at Bristol. But there's one bit of the dullard which has stuck with me: he wrote a book, *Remarks on Colour*, based on Goethe (flee, flee). How can I know that you, or anyone else, sees colour the same way as me? Is my red the same as yours?

If you ever did see the same colours as me, I'm pretty sure you don't now. Optic Neuritis. It's one of the symptoms. Not only is everything blurred or double, it's all rather washed out too. Whereas colours seemed vivid before, now they rarely are. A bit East German if you will, rather boring-looking.

Combined with my tremoring hand, bad eyesight is a modern day disaster. Even a five-word text takes me hours. 'With you in two minutes' is not a message I can honestly send. But there's one upside to this vision thing – I really like black-and-white TV now. When I was sharing a room in Bristol with my mate P, we had a tiny b-&-w set to watch *Hill Street Blues* and *Neighbours* on. Even then, telly controllers were hugely biased towards colour. About the only b-&-w programme one could see were the fantastic Sunday evening *Bilko* repeats. Not even they are on the Beeb anymore; they'd rather show that awful Dick van Dyke doctor-detective stuff than black-and-white TV gems like *The Twilight Zone*. Do they still sell cheapo black-and-white TV licenses? Could I persuade the kids to downgrade?

47 Card
Thursday 19 June

It was my wedding anniversary this week, so a card was needed. There's one fabbo card shop in Cambridge, so I buggied off there. But, crap! There was a three inch step to get in. I tried. Honest. But the buggy couldn't make. The shop didn't have a ramp. Fortunately, they had a card with a pug on it on display, so I was able to make my purchase by pointing, pleading, and with only a few grazes and profuse thank yous, I was back home with the card.

Slavey 18-year old has now finished her A Levels, so is available to hold a pen for me and inscribe the 20th card. Then it was off to Suffolk for an anniversary meal by the seaside.

The buggy couldn't make much headway by the sea, but we were able to have a lovely meal and watch our beloved Chile thrash Spain at football, so it was an altogether lovely anniversary – pug card, potted shrimps, Chile victory. What more could you need?

48 Coffee
Wednesday 25 June

Just to re-emphasise, for any who didn't get it first time, I am NOT in pain. This thing is boring, tedious, frightening etc. But painful it ain't. Falling over is painful, but I haven't done that in days. So I don't hurt today. I hate pain and am as much a wimp as anyone. But I don't have any. Got it?

You find yourself drinking a lot of coffee. I rather like coffee, but there's a limit. My Cambridge days are filled by Starbucks, Nero, Costa, Hot Numbers and CB2. Flat white, cappuccino, latte. Instant or ground, at £2.50 a pop. When you live off benefits, these things add up. When did it get so pricey?

Here in Essex, I drink even more of it. My dad is making me a cup now, which reminds me that coffee is a diuretic too; none too helpful when I'm miles from the loo. But the real story about coffee is that it makes me feel just a bit better, more normal. It doesn't help me speak, or walk, or see. But it does cheer me up – a damn sight more than that yucky green tea which R wants me to take. Long-Suffering Wife thinks I drink too much of it, and she's doubtless right. But I like it and along with the cigs, I'm in no hurry to stop.

All gone a bit quiet on the stem cell front. J has given me a start date of December 1 for the re-injection, but that sounds miles off; like the nearest loo, given my current decline. Who gives a stuff? It's sunny and my mug is brimming.

49 Bosoms
Sunday 29 June

I have never never been a fan of huge, Jordan type pneumatic tits. But with my eyesight so rubbish, and me down here on this buggy, about four foot tall, I've changed my mind. The bigger the hooters, the better. Preferably under a super-tight shiny sweater.

Here in this part of Cambridge, the pavements are narrow. Overtaking or being passed is tricky at the best of times.

And when you've got Optic Neuritis and a tremor in your head, it isn't the best of times. Add in the trend for loose fitting tops, and there may be trouble.

When people ask, I often say that I can't see. Simple, but untrue. I can see. I just see weirdly. It's like one of those old comedy silents, shot at 12 frames a second rather than 25, where all movement is jerky and disconnected. Everything is blurred and double too.

The upshot is that I can go out. I do go out. But I also make mistakes. Stupid, humiliating mistakes. I pay effusive thanks for the lovely meal – to a coffee machine. And the commonest boob (apols etc) is directional. I can't tell whether someone else on the same pavement is coming towards me or walking away. Collisions are frequent, as people tend to look the same to me, front or back.

Unless it's a woman with big tits.

50
Friday 4 July

It is coming. I am ready. No I'm not. Yes, I am. I've had one flipping year to prepare and have done quite a lot, viz:

> Written a will
> Posted a Living Will to my GP
> Visited the hospice
> Applied for life insurance failed, chiz
> Been to exotic places a lot with my buggy, to Morocco, Thailand,
> Cape Town, Essex.
> Had good chats with Long Suffering Wife and kids.

As a rank amateur on medical stuff, I assume that I won't get my final infection or whatever till it turns a bit colder, autumn or something, but I am as ready as I will be. Probably.

Today, 4th of July, is a huge deal. For Yanks. And Bill Paxton fans. 30 years ago, along with 2 mates, P and E, between Eton and Bristol, I took a Gap Year trip to the USA. Incredible though it may sound these days, I hadn't really been abroad much. Not even to Spain. Suffolk, yes. Only the bare minimum essentials were in our luggage: black tie suits, Barbours etc. After one day in New York Port Authority Bus Terminal, we concluded that America was not ready for us.

I did have a list of US emergency phone numbers provided by ML, a friend of my then girlfriend, who I had once met in Paris, so I dialled the top number, which was for her family on an island near Baltimore.

We stayed with them for about 3 months.

This week, one of ML's brothers, R, came to London. P, E and me had supper with him. We Skyped ML and his mother. BA. They were all just as lovely as 30 years ago. R invited Slavey 18-year-old daughter and her boyfriend to stay on her upcoming Gap year trip to South America and California.

What goes around comes around. Yes, I'm ready.

51 Stem Cell War
Wednesday 9 July

It all sounds so lovely and cuddly. Newton, Faraday, Bohr, Darwin.

Isn't science friendly? Afraid not. It's preening, arrogant, defensive, hostile to change. Like everything else. Like TV, which I know much more about.

When I was making *A Week in Politics* for Channel 4, most of us on the team would religiously watch *On The Record* on the Beeb, all the better to rubbish its failings. It was the same at *Newsnight*, at which Channel 4 News was our target.

Harmless games? Isn't a little arrogance rather sweet? Think again: ask any Brazilian football fan, after that 7-1 drubbing[1]. All that Samba swagger booted away with 4 German goals in 6 minutes.

Of course I'm parti-pris on this; we're talking about my survival for cripes sake. I'm not THAT nice etc! But the reaction of almost everyone in the neuro world to my Stem Cell thingy keeps me up even more than this tremor.

One example. My lovely Essex neurologist G is battling with my lovely stem cell guy J over the MRI I need. What sort of magnet, how good an image, just brain or spinal cord too? We can, probably, pay a grand for a private one. But I've got a kind mother; most people can't pay.

They rely on people like us to do things first, and it's so flipping hard. Or people get trampled on, like Henrietta Lacks[2] (note for dimbos not in TV: do keep up, read the book etc).

So who's right? The lovely neurologist (supported by the lovely MS nurse, M, who visited yesterday) or the lovely stem cell people?
Answer is a total copout; they both are.

One way or another, E and J will help me to make this happen, or I'm a Brazilian goalie. Maybe it'll fail; doubtless it will. But maybe it'll work. Either way, we will have learned something. That's how it works. Or should.

---

[1]Brazil's defeat, on home-ground, in the 2014 World Cup semi-finals was a national humiliation.
[2]Henrietta Lacks was an African American woman whose cancer cells were used for medical research following a tumour biopsy, without her permission. The cells were cultured and created the HeLa cell line, the first human immortal cell line

52 Socks
Thursday 10 July

I have always hated the last bit of getting dressed in the morning. The socks.

Long-Suffering Wife and I went to London today for a swanky lunch – a birthday present from my kind friend S, so had to ask the Carer to find some. But I fear socks. The fact that I have to get someone else to put them on for me doesn't make it better.

The problem goes back years. As a boy, I always hated making stupid mistakes, showing myself up as a twit. And so the socks problem arose: maybe there's a left sock and a right sock. Maybe everyone knows. Everyone but me, and they are too polite to mention that I'VE GOT MY SOCKS THE WRONG WAY ROUND! Any fool can see that! Any fool but me. And they are all sniggering about it.

So I used to spend hours inspecting the contents of my drawer for the L and R which I KNEW must be printed somewhere on each sock, if I only knew where to look.

The swanky meal was great. I've promised L-S W that I'd take her to the Caprice for 20 plus years – but never have. The S offer for my birthday completely exhausted my excuses. It was great: even with my socks on wrong.

53 Trust
Monday 14 July

I know that a lot of you would deny my preparedness for what is to come. I won't claim to have discovered a magic formula or anything. But it works for me.

It's trust. I trust Long-Suffering Wife. I trust my MS nurse, M, who insists that I am a 7.5, not an 8.5. I trust my Stem Cell friend, E. I trust my parents, here in Essex. I don't trust the Argentine defence, but so what?

A problem shared is a problem halved, they say. Most of what 'they say' is cobblers – based on Green Tea and not smoking – but this one has the advantage of also being true. So here's my Top Tip: trust and share.

It's quite a burden, to be trusted by someone dying. I see that. But it makes the unbearable bearable. You won't even be there for much of the pain.

55 Farewell NCIS
Wednesday 16 July

I'll be leaving Essex for the last time shortly. The building work, finally, is pretty much done and I want to return to Long-Suffering Wife and the kids as soon as. Even with help from the council, we are totally broke now, and living on paltry benefits – so city living, here I come. New wheelchair still not come, but buggy will do for the moment, so long as I don't do too much indoor crash damage with my awful driving.

But there are things I'll miss, of course. My thoughtful parents, their licky dogs, cool garden. The TV always on, showing some US detective dross like *Murder She Wrote* or *NCIS*. Whereas in Cambridge our snobby viewing centres on Channels 2 and 4, Essex is much more 5 or 3 (or 1, for *Bargain Hunt* or *Shaun The Sheep*).

It has been hideously hot and, as I wrote from Thailand, hot weather is bad news with MS. My tremor has moved into my head, so my eyesight is even worse than normal.

56 Bed
Monday 21 July

A truly sickening image when I turned on the news yesterday. Rolf Harris, shot from behind, cuddling a prepubescent girl. Vile. Then the commentary began.

The old beardie geezer was Australian, true. He and his 13-year-old granddaughter are the only family survivors after MH17*. Oops. Tie me kangaroo down.

I spend most of my time abed these days, and fall out loads trying to transfer from bed to buggy or back. Often builders, summoned by my cries for help, have had to forego their vital task (drinking tea), pick me up and deposit me back under the duvet. So the Occupational Therapy department from Addenbrooke's have come up with a wheeze which should help: a mattress lifty thing.

It has long been a worry, both from me and from Long-Suffering Wife, that our house, with all these adaptations, might end up looking too hospital-y. The kids, anxious that nobody must view us as 'the freak family', must have been horrified when a baseball-capped engineer arrived and started fiddling under my bed.

But it's ok, I think. And bloody amazing. From lying in bed, I press a yellow button, and hey! I'm sitting! The machinery is invisible, the effect life-changing. I'm up, I'm in the buggy, ready for the day.

Stem cell news: there isn't any. I am gonna get the MRI at some point. But still no UK doctor, either to harvest or to re-inject. Ed and Jorgen are working madly, Rob has offered to flog his beautiful Thai hotel to pay for it all, Sue has looked for investors. But nada just yet. But a cool bed gizmo makes up for it. Almost.

*Malaysian Airlines flight MH17, en route from Amsterdam to Kuala Lumpar, was shot down over Ukraine on Thursday 17 July

57 Modafinil
Friday 25 July

Sadly, it's not the wonder-drug which some papers – like *The Guardian* or *The Indy* – seemed to suggest. Nor does it make you brainy, as many internet searches suggest. It doesn't help my tremor at all – I still hit the wrong keys all the time. It is flipping hard to get, illegal and very expensive. But it does one thing, and it does it well. I am in a cafe, writing this at 11.00am, and I might be in bed. And it's thanks to that filthy-tasting pill I swallowed an hour ago. For, despite the efforts of the NHS, I can say with confidence: MODAFINIL KEEPS ME AWAKE.

I didn't take one yesterday because
a) they cost a fortune and
b) my good friend, SoC, was visiting, and a chippy harangue from her Millie Tant
   northern accent would waken anything, dead or alive, and
c) I had loads of coffee. And Coke
But it didn't work. Zzzz

Our story begins more a year ago. My sleep was crappy, 2 hours max at night, most of the day. I was keeping people up all night, with trips to the horrid loo of our rented flat. I had heard, and read, an awful lot about this miraculous potion that students take during essay crises to stay alert. So I asked for some. Big mistake.

Because (I assume) of all those students and geeks are taking it, Modafinil cannot be easily prescribed. Not by my MS nurse. not by my GP. It takes some sort of expert. A sleep specialist, perhaps.

Cambridge is THE PLACE to be ill, they say (although we still haven't found a medic to try my Stem Cell thingy, and I'm up against the clock, arses). Cambridge even boasts THE guru for this disease, The Great Compston, and I've got an appointment with TGC in a few weeks. Anyhow, being so groovy, we even have a sleep clinic in Papworth nearby, and in my quest for Modafinil, that's where I went next.

I apologise in advance to those of you with 'clever' spam filters or bandwidth problems (BBC staff, mostly). But I love this picture.

I was wired up, plugged in and shown to a room. Suffice it to say, I didn't sleep much, with all those wires and the urgent need to pee. I eagerly anticipated my Modafinil. But no. Instead of focussing on my daytime sleepiness, they wanted only to discuss my nighttime wakefulness, and the 'restless leg syndrome'. So I got a prescription. Not for the Modafinil I wanted, but for a pretty futile Parkinson's drug, Gabapentin. So I've got even more pills (9 a day!) to remember, and still no Modafinil.
So I get it – at 100 quid a time – off the internet, sent illegally from India and Hong Kong.

67

58 Scrounge
Tuesday 29 July

It may not sound a huge deal. I may be wrong, unlikely as it sounds. But I'm pretty sure. I AM NO WORSE TODAY THAN YESTERDAY.

For the past age, I have had to spend much of my energy in getting used to a new me. But not today. No better, mind, but no worse. And that means, perhaps, that I have found some sort of plateau. A crappy plateau, maybe, like Suffolk. But a plateau.

The benefits agency has assigned me a work coach, Gwen, thanks, I assume, to the oh-so-lovely Quiet Man who vows to get us scroungers off benefits and into work. The bleedin' Quiet Man [Iain Duncan Smith, aka IDS][1] is on the radio right now, banging on to WatO [The World at One] listeners. Turn down the volume, IDS.

There is one fun part of this work coach thing. I've now been put into a 'team', under poor Gwen, who will teach us the skills we'll need in the world of work. Another groovy IDS wheeze? What skills will Gwen have up her sleeve for a TV journalist who can only use one finger? Raffia? Hasn't the Mrs Lovejoy award for raffia work already gone? Or maybe there's more.

I can't wait.

There are, they say, two things that nobody can avoid. It was the other one which dominated yesterday as Long-Suffering Wife filled in my Tax Return for me (Cos I can't hold a pen. Gwen[2]). It was easy. It used to take me days! Too easy, surely. Yet another plus for being a jobless cripple! Doubtless a scrounger, eh IDS?

[1] Tory Secretary of State for Work and Pensions, 2010-2016.
[2] Gwen wrote an apologetic letter, having been added by Charlie to his email blog list, telling him he would never need to attend a work coach meeting with her.

59 Stem Cell Part 94
Sunday 3 August

A pols to those seeking belly laughs. This one will be more newsy than funny. Normal service soon.

Up here in Scotland while builders finish in Cambridge. No road works on A9 for the first time ever – doubtless something to do with upcoming Salmond heroic failure. I wonder if England would end stupid clocks going back in winter if Scotland voted yes: we were always told that we had to endure GMT to protect Scottish school kids. Hmm...

Now for the duller stuff. First, I should emphasise and reinforce any scepticism you might have. It probably won't work, so don't feel bad if your end can't work. So be it.

However, I have divvied up the tasks cos it helps to remember. At the same time, Long-Suffering Wife and were struck by a warning from M, my lovely MS nurse. She warned that desperate people – like us – tend to make terrible judgements. I'm sure she's right; I fancied Chile for the World Cup. With that in mind, L-S W and I have walked away from decision-making and handed it on to the efficient, analytical and frankly scary SoC. So here goes a list without either of our names on it.

The MRI will be overseen by Giles, be private in Colchester and paid for by my kind mum. The harvesting will be done by some medic prepared to see off the attack dogs of the GMC, Rob will be working with SoC on finding one who categorises me as a compassionate case. September.

The harvested marrow then goes to Canada where Ed and Jorgen will oversee the Novagenesis geniuses who will magic it into stem cells: October-November.

The lovely stem cells will be re-introduced by injecting them into my spine or brain (I forget) in December.

By Christmas, I'm cured etc. and Novagenesis win Nobel prize and get made Time people of the year, Gillian wins hateful of Baftas, RTS awards, Oscars etc.

Novagenesis magic will cost a jazillion packets. Sue Douglas will advise on how to get that. Is that understandable? Sorry if it's boring, but loads of people wanted to know. I'll be funny again soon.

60 Dudes
Tuesday 5 August

It looks piss-easy. Kinda cool, sometimes. One flick of the wrist, and the dude is off, racing off, ducking, diving, doing wheelies? I'm sure it is like that for some. But that takes years of practice. For novices like me, wheelchairs are effing hard work and impossible to control, forwards, backwards, anything.

There are two types of chair, essentially. Manual wheelchairs, like this one I'm sitting in now, have metal bits, parallel to each wheel, which can be pushed back, forward, slow, etc, for maximum dude-tricks and skilful wheelies etc. The chairs are light, fold up small, and are easy to transport in a car e.g. up here to northwest Scotland.

But manual chairs have disadvantages too. This one has no foot-rests cos I fell on them and bust them. You need to have equal strength in both arms to be able to go straight; with a weaker left than right, I naturally veer and look totally undude-esque. And the whole palaver is bloody hard work for an indolent arse like me.

Back in Cambridge, my buggy awaits. I love my buggy; it's been with me everywhere (Thailand, South Africa, Morocco etc.). But it, too, has a downside. It weighs a bleeding ton, falls on top of me a lot, is hard to get in a car and, as the crumbling Cambridge walls can attest, has the handy turning circle of a pregnant rhino.

When we get back to Cambridge next week, there should be a groovy compromise waiting. My OT advisor, L, has, after a year's waiting, finally got the NHS to stump up for a new chair with an on-a-sixpence turn. It's costing them, you, a packet. It'll be amazing, I hope. But I'm sure I'll find some cunning new way of misusing it and continuing my journey to un-dude-dom.

Sunday 31 August

L ucre, lolly, cash, wonga, money, dosh.

In the world of work, you want to amass loads. In this topsy-turvy-land of benefits, by contrast, you want none. Indeed, you are frequently checked to ascertain that you haven't any salted away. Having spent the lot on our house adaptations (pics attached, usual apols to those with tedious BBC spam filters) and with me un-earning a bean in 2014, ought to be a breeze. But it still took ages, and was only the beginning.

Take today. Or rather, don't. Not good. It started with me burning Long Suffering Wife's favourite blanket, and has been downhill since.

But that's another story. Money is our topic today. I need an eye kept on me, otherwise I do stupid things like burning a blanket. L-S W often needs to go out on weekdays, so I need to employ a carer. And here's the rub. We need to prove our poverty by convincing a council 'long-term care assessor' of our situation.

The long-term care assessor, Clare, was friendly, asked the usual questions about medicines, allergies, hospital trips etc. I answered as best I could, though I am impossible to understand by late in the afternoon. Now we wait. More.

62 Temporary
Wednesday 13 August

Sorry this comes so hot on the heels of the last. Its just that this chair business was today. No more for a week, promise.

There's a difference, and it's huge. To you, a bloke in a wheelchair is just that. Poor guy. But look again. Broken leg? Spina Bifida? How does he treat the chair? With callousness or reverence? It's important, because the answer to that might well tell you an awful lot.

I got a new wheelchair today. Ostensibly its great. Turns on a sixpence, gets me anywhere, easily. It tilts, whirrs, zooms. I hate it.

I loved my buggy. It was bashed up, yes. Bits fell off regularly. The armrests were wonky, true. Screws were missing. But maybe that's why I loved it. It was temporary, a phase. This one seems much more permanent, and i hate that. It might as well have, in ginormous letters 'this arse will never, ever, walk again'.

On the Stem Cell front, I'm booked in for 3 MRI scans next week. Then an appointment with The Great Compston on Friday, at which he'll doubtless throw buckets of cold water over the whole thing.

Tuesday 19 August

So we're off at last. 3 MRI scans in one session; brain, t-spine, c-spine (whatever they are.) But this bit of the stem cell thingy was done privately, kindly paid for with my mother's credit card, so was in the swanky private hospital in Colchester. Arrived – as is my mother's way – half an hour early and settled ourselves by reception. A menu for all-day paninis was displayed, and a series of closed cream-beige doors. Then it was my turn. The two friendly radiographers eyed my wheelchair suspiciously.

"Can you walk?" one asked.

"No."

"Not even a few steps?"

"No. Not even one."

"Well you can't bring that in. Magnets, you see."

We trooped through the hospital, out to a car park and to a lorry marked 'Mobile MRI.' My glasses, phone and fags were removed and – leaning on my poor mother – I got out of my chair and mounted the bed. An ice-hockey mask thing was secured over my face, I was given some ear plugs, and lay down.

It's fourteen years since my last MRI, but they haven't got any quieter. It sounds like a zillion midges, attacking the Chinese Ping-Pong team. Zzzz plonk zzzz zzzz plonk plonk plonk etc. For ninety minutes.

"Keep totally still please. Your neck next." Meanwhile, clutching her unfeasibly large cheque book, my mother went back to reception to pay her ginormous bill.

The scans will go to G in about 10 days. To tell him what he knows already. Meanwhile, I'm to Addenbrooke's on Friday for my hugely important appointment with The Great Compston. Wish me luck.

Wednesday 20 August

I worked with DF for years. No surprise, then, that we got quite a lot of guests done.

I was told years ago by a maker of cool documentaries that she kept a list of boastable previous guests, the better to bribe others to appear. By the programme's end, my boast list was pretty cool and I've attached it to this to impress.

The point of all this is serendipity. One name on the list is Phil Zimbardo, psychologist creator of the Stamford Prison Experiment (Wikipedia for those not in telly). In advance of the interview, I sat down on a train (Liverpool St to Kelvedon) to read Phil's latest book, which compared his Stamford 'prison' to Abu Ghraib in Iraq. I read, as I did back then, pretty speedily, and moved to turn the page. A fat finger from my neighbour jabbed into the book and prevented me.

"I haven't finished yet." American accent. Maybe that explained the effing rudeness. "Hi, we haven't met yet. I'm Rob. I was the chief interrogator at Abu Ghraib Prison." Arresting line!

We had a cool conversation, Rob and I. We had lunch with SoC. He had groovy plans for interview rooms, where to sit, wall colours etc. He agreed to meet with Phil and to let us film it. DF died before I could set it up. Damn.

Moral : carpe diem, dudes. Particularly if you work in telly.

DF in my glasses on a flight from New York

64 and a half boast list

1. Presidents

Asif Ali Zardari
President of Pakistan
Hamid Karzai
President of Afghanistan
Lula da Silva
President of Brazil
Omar Al-Bashir
President of Sudan
Evo Morales
President of Bolivia
Michelle Bachelet
President of Chile
Daniel Ortega
President of Nicaragua
Shimon Peres
President of Israel
Yoweri Museveni
President of Uganda
Paul Kagame
President of Rwanda
Jose Manuel Barroso
President of the EU Commission
Ernest Koroma
President of Sierra Leone
Mikheil Saakashvili
President of Georgia
Abdullah Yusuf Ahmed
President of Somalia
Ellen Johnson-Sirleaf
President of Liberia
Jose Ramos-Horta
President of East Timor
Toomas Henrik Ilves
President of Estonia
Fatmir Sejdiu
President of Kosovo
Alvaro Uribe
President of Colombia
Juan Manuel Santos
President of Colombia
Danilo Turk
President of Slovenia
Tarja Halonen
President of Finland

Victor Yuschenko
President of Ukraine
Mehmet Talat
President of Northern Cyprus
Serzh Sargasian
President of Armenia
Sheikh Sharif Sheikh
Ahmed   *President of Somalia*
Allesane Ouattara
President of Ivory Coast
Ilham Aliyev
President of Azerbaijan
Michael D Higgins
President of Ireland
Ivo Josipovic
President of Croatia

2. Prime Ministers

Tony Blair
PM of UK
Gordon Brown
PM of UK
David Cameron
PM of UK
Morgan Tsvangirai
PM of Zimbabwe
Raila Odinga
PM of Kenya
Ismael Haniya
PM of Palestine
Recep Tayyip Erdogan
PM of Turkey
Abhisit Vejjajiva
PM of Thailand
Salam Fayyad
PM of Palestine
Spencer Baldwin
PM of Antigua
Shaukat Aziz
PM of Pakistan
Agim Ceku
PM of Kosovo
Helen Clark
PM of New Zealand

Sheikh Hasina Wazed
PM of Bangladesh
Meles Zenawi
PM of Ethiopia
Matti VanHannen
PM of Finland
Nikoloz Gilauri
PM of Georgia
Fakhruddin Ahmed
PM of Bangladesh
Sein Win
PM in Exile of Burma
Yusuf Raza Gilani
PM of Pakistan
John Key
PM of New Zealand
Julia Gillard
PM of Australia
Laurence Gonzi
PM of Malta
Hamad bin Jassim al Thani
PM of Qatar
Jean-Claude Juncker
PM of Luxembourg
Abdiweli Mohamed Ali
PM of Somalia
Jyrki Katainen
PM of Finland
Mihai Razvan Ungureanu
PM of Romania

3. Former Presidents and PMs

Vaclav Havel
Former President of Czech Republic
Benazir Bhutto
Former PM of Pakistan
in both of the above
cases, this was their last
international interview
Binyamin Netanyahu
Former PM of Israel
Sheikh Hasina Wazed
Former PM of Bangladesh

Nawaz Sharif
Former PM of Pakistan
John Major
Former PM of United Kingdom
FW De Klerk
Former President of South Africa
Mikhail Gorbachev
Former President of the Soviet Union
Mary Robinson
Former President of Ireland
Wilfried Martens
Former PM of Belgium
Alejandro Toledo
Former President of Peru
Martti Ahtissari
Former President of Finland
Olusegun Obasanjo
Former President of Nigeria
Mahathir bin Mohamad
Former PM of Malaysia
Pervez Musharraf
Former President of Pakistan
Carl Bildt
Former PM of Sweden
Bertie Ahern
Former PM of Ireland
George HW Bush
Former President of the USA
Miklos Nemeth
Former PM of Hungary
Ricardo Lagos
Former President of Chile
Jose Maria Aznar
Former PM of Spain
Ayad Allawi
Former PM of Iraq
Ejup Ganic
Former President of Bosnia-Herzegovina
John Bruton
Former PM of Ireland
Michel Rocard
Former PM of France
Dominique de Villepin
Former PM of France
George Papandreou
Former PM of Greece

4. Foreign Ministers
Sam Kutesa
FM, Uganda
Jorge Taiana
FM, Argentina
Rohitha Bogollagama
FM, Sri Lanka
Rangin Dadfar Spanta
FM, Afghanistan
Michael Frendo
FM, Malta
Noer Hasan Wirajuda
FM, Indonesia
Vuk Jeremic
FM, Serbia
Makhdoom Shah
Mahmood Qureshi
FM, Pakistan
Ossur Skarphendinsson
FM, Iceland
David Miliband
FM, UK
Pranab Mukherjee
FM, India
Jose Garcia Belaunde
FM, Peru
Nasser Judeh
FM, Jordan
Alex Stubb
FM, Finland
Abu Baker al-Qerbi
FM, Yemen
Marty Natalegawa
FM, Indonesia
William Hague
FM, UK
Carl Bildt
FM, Sweden
Rene Castro
FM, Costa Rica
Khalid Bin Ahmed Al Khalif
FM, Bahrain
Franco Frattini
FM, Italy
Ali Ahmed Karti
FM, Sudan
Reginald Bosquet
FM, St Lucia
Karel Schwarzenberg
FM, Czech Rep

Erkki Tuomioja
FM, Finland
Hina Rabbani Khar
FM, Pakistan
Hina Rabbani Khar
FM, Pakistan

5. Political leaders
General David Petraeus
ISAF Commander in Afghanistan
Mullah Zaeef
Taliban founder
Ban Ki Moon
UN Secretary General
Jacob Zuma
President, ANC
Morgan Tsvangirai
Leader, MDC of Zimbabwe
James Baker +
Lee Hamilton
US Iraq report authors
Donald Rumsfeld
Former US Defence Secretary
Francisco Calderon
Vice-President of Colombia
Walid Jumblatt
Leader, Druze Party of Lebanon
Imran Khan
Leader, Movement for Justice Party of Pakistan
Gerry Adams
Leader, Sinn Fein party of Northern Ireland
John Bolton
Former US ambassador to UN
Comrade Guarav
Leader, Maoist insurgency in Nepal
Peter Mandelson
European Commissioner for Trade
Eduard Limonov
Leader, Bolshevik Party of Russia
Madeleine Albright
Former US Secretary of State
Abdullah Abdullah
Opposition Presidential Candidate, Afghanistan
General Wesley Clark
Former NATO Supreme allied commander Europe

Ali Allawi
Former defence minister, Iraq
David Cameron
UK leader of the Opposition
Evgeny Lebedev
Newspaper proprietor
Mo Ibrahim
Philanthropist
Wangari Maathai
Nobel laureate
Tahir El-Faki
*Chair, Legislative council, JEM
Rebels in Darfur*
Chris Patten
Last Governor of Hong Kong
Jean Ping
Chair, African Union Commission
Archbishop Desmond Tutu
Nobel Peace Prizewinner
Robert Gates
US Secretary for Defense
Karen Abu Zayd
*Commissioner-General, UN
Refugee Agency*
Rev. Al Sharpton
Civil Rights Campaigner
Don McKinnon
Secretary-General, Commonwealth
Henry Kissinger
Former US Secretary of State
David Trimble
Nobel Peace Prizewinner
Ian Paisley
First Minister of Northern Ireland
Gwede Mantashe
Secretary-General, ANC
Josette Sheeran
Director, World Food Programme
Nafie Ali Nafie
*Chief Sudanese negotiator in
Darfur*
Rodolphe Adada
*Joint UN-AU Special
Representative in Darfur*
Luis-Moreno Ocampo
*Chief Prosecutor, International
Criminal Court*
Zbigniew Brezezinski
*Former US National Security
Advisor*

Arthur Mutambara
*Leader, MDC Mutambara,
Zimbabwe*
Boutros Boutros-Ghali
Former UN Secretary-General
Jesse Jackson
Former US presidential candidate
Rudy Giuliani
Former Mayor of New York
Chaturon Chaisang
Former Deputy PM of Thailand
Javier Solana
Chair, EU Council
Amr Moussa
Secretary-General, Arab League
Mohammed
Waheed Hassan
Vice-President, The Maldives
John Kerry
Former US Presidential Candidate
General John Craddock
*NATO Supreme Allied
Commander, Europe*
Kamal Nath
*Commerce & Industry Minister
of India*
Bill Gates
*Philanthropist & Microsoft
Founder*
Christine Lagarde
Finance Minister of France
John McCain
Former US Presidential candidate
Anders Fogh Rasmussen
NATO Secretary-General
Sheikha Mozah
Campaigner
Shirin Ebadi
*Iranian Nobel Peace Prizewinner
and Human Rights Lawyer*
Michael Chertoff
*Former US Secretary for Homeland
Security*
Fernando Dos Santos
Finance Minister of Portugal
Helen Clark
Head of UNDP
Wyclef Jean
Haitian Presidential Candidate

Ingrid Betancourt
Former FARC Hostage
Antonio Guterres
Head of UNHCR
Dr. Yahya al Mantheri
Chairman, State Council of Oman
Ambassador William Swing
*D-G, International Organisation
for Migration*
Mohammed El Senussi
Crown Prince of Libya
Michelle Bachelet
Executive Director, UN Women
Munib Al Masri
Palestinian Legislative Councillor
Babatunde Osotimehin
Head of UN Population Fund
Ibrahim Gambari
Head of UNAMID
Filippo Grandi
Head of UNWRA
Doug Wead
*Senior adviser to Ron Paul
Presidential Campaign*
Dennis Ross
*Former Chief White House adviser
on Middle East*
Suha Arafat
Widow
Gene Robinson
US Episcopalian Bishop

6. Film directors and Actors
George Clooney
Director + Actor
Quentin Tarantino
Director
Robert De Niro
Actor
Helen Mirren
Actor
Juliette Binoche
Actor
Saffron Burrows
Actor
Anil Kapoor
Actor
John Hurt

Actor
Michael Caine
Actor
Khalid Abdallah
Actor
Wim Wenders
Director
Rob Reiner
Director
Gene Wilder
Actor
Oliver Stone
Director
Richard Eyre
Director
Shilpa Shetty
Bollywood actress
Kevin MacDonald
Director
Michael Sheen
Actor
Bill Nighy
Actor
John Hannah
Actor
John Kani
Actor/Writer
Geena Davis
Actor
James Ivory
Director
Colin Firth
Actor
Ron Howard
Director
Danny DeVito
Actor
Ridley Scott
Director
Stockard Channing
Actor
Mia Farrow
Actor and UNICEF ambassador
Stephen Daldry
Director
Danny Boyle
Director
Will Ferrell
Actor
Jeremy Irons

Actor
Roberto Benigni
Actor
Amitabh Bachchan
Bollywood Actor
Werner Herzog
Director
Juliette Lewis
Actor
Omid Djalili
Actor
Samantha Bond
Actor
Simon Callow
Actor
Alejandro González Iñárritu
Director
Catherine Deneuve
Actor
Anthony Hopkins
Actor
Matthew Fox
Actor
Olivia Williams
Actor
Geoffrey Rush
Actor
Cuba Gooding Junior
Actor
Vanessa Redgrave
Actor
Sarah Jessica Parker
Actor
Stephen Soderburgh
Director
Emma Thompson
Actor and Screenwriter
Robin Williams
Actor
Elijah Wood
Actor
Viggo Mortensen
Actor
Christina Ricci
Actor
Patrick Stewart
Actor

7 .Musicians, artists and performers
Andrew Lloyd-Webber
Roger Daltrey
Dionne Warwick
Sophie Ellis-Bextor
Beverley Knight
Jean Michel Jarre
Daniel Barenboim
Annie Lennox
Manu Chao
Hugh Masakela
Tony Banks + Mike
Rutherford (Genesis)
Tim Rice
Sergio Mendes
Bryan Adams
Jane Birkin
Jay Sean
Lang Lang
Carlos Acosta
Yoko Ono
Chris Rea
David Hasselhoff
Mark Knopfler
Roger Waters
Esperanza Spalding
Billy Connolly
Joan Armatrading
Angela Giorgihou
James Blunt
Sting
Michael Flatley
Paloma Faith
Eddie Izzard
Ruby Wax
Alicia Keys
Peter Gabriel
Lenny Kravitz
Emili Sande
Kate Nash
Gilbert and George
Gary Lightbody
Noel Gallagher

7. Sportspeople

Lewis Hamilton
Motor Racing driver
Chris Bonington
Mountaineer
Shane Warne
Cricketer
Ben Johnson
Athlete / Drug cheat
Ian Botham
Cricketer
Garry Kasparov
Chess Grandmaster
Steve Redgrave
Rower
Francois Pienaar
Rugby Player
Aaron Mokoene
Footballer
Martina Navratilova
Tennis Player
Jenson Button
Racing Driver
Oscar Pistorious
Paralympic athlete
Michael Vaughan
Cricketer
Roger Federer
Tennis Player
David Campese
Rugby Player
Carl Lewis
Athlete
Sam Waley-Cohen
Jockey
Juan Martin Del Potro
Tennis Player
Novak Djokovic
Tennis Player
Bernie Ecclestone
Motor Racing magnate
Sebastian Coe
Athlete
Eric Cantona
Footballer

8. Writers and Campaigners

Julian Assange
Tina Brown
Ian McEwan
Bob Geldof
Gore Vidal
Freddie Forsyth
John Pilger
Jacqueline Wilson
Mario Vargas Llosa
Christopher Hitchens
Naomi Klein
Bjorn Lomborg
Nicholas Taleb
Irshad Manji
Ben Elton
Louis de Bernieres
Isabel Allende
Sebastian Faulks
Armando Iannucci
Terry Pratchett
Steven Johnson
Gillian Slovo
Simon Singh
David Aaronovitch
Michael Sandel
Eoin Colfer
Dambisa Moyo
Andrew Rawnsley
Lucy Prebble
Fatima Bhutto
Andrew Roberts
Alain de Botton
John Simpson
Martin Jacques
PJ O'Rourke
George Monbiot
Bob Woodward
Kate and Gerry McCann
Hugh Fearnley-Whittingstall
Michael Connolly
Amos Oz
Anthony Horowitz
Paul Krugman

9. Scientists

Craig Venter
Geneticist
Robert Winston
Fertility surgeon
Phil Zimbardo
Psychologist
Margaret Chan
Director, World Health Organisation
John Ellis
Director, CERN
Martin Rees
Astronomer Royal
James Lovelock
Environmental theorist
Michio Kaku
Physicist
Heston Blumenthal
Chef
Jimmy Wales
Founder of Wikipedia
Buzz Aldrin
Astronaut
James Watson
Co-discoverer of DNA structure

[Charlie begins to make more mistakes in his writing from now on.
They have been left in deliberately.]

65
Friday 22 August*

This is a crap email to write but needs must.

There are three people I trust on MS matters, G, M and The Great Compston: and all 3 have now given the thumbs down to Novagenesis. It's time to throw in the towel (for those following this in order, number 13 is about where things change. Return to 13, like Snakes and Ladders).

By the way, TGC is looking even deeper into Novagenesis, so all this COULD change.

So its thanks time. Thanks and apologies, and shame.
I want to thank Ed and Rob and Sarah and Sue and my mum. You have all contributed so so much and I want it on record that you could not have done ANY more.

I also want to thank those of YOU who sent me messages of support ahead of today's meeting.

But most of all I want to thank my Long-Suffering Wife.
It's getting bad; even with just one finger, typing is shitty.
Over and out.
Cx

*Written after the long-awaited appointment with Professor Compston at Addenbrooke's

66 Transfers
Monday 15 September

Sorry to be back, everyone. Driven to this by watching News 24 weather report for the zillionth time today…

But lying in bed doing naff all is boring as hell and makes typing – even with one finger, wrong hand – seem an exciting option by comparison. I have three broken ribs (7, 8, 10 for those who understand this nonsense) and it hurts like nobody's business. Plus, it's dull.

The 'carer' came and fixed my lunch – a sandwich, half eleven! – and then pissed off, thankfully, muttering to herself about my 'bobs'/'private areas'/'other' or whatever her word is today.

Then another visitor. OT, (occupational therapy) with a 'transfer board'. They call it that, you may well prefer the technical jargon, 'plank'. It's a flat bit of wood, looking a bit like a shove ha'penny board, that I use to slide between bed and wheelchair. Using it should prevent more falls, more broken bones. How much are we, you, paying for that plank? Nothing against it. It's a good plank, a premium plank. No splinters, attractive etc. But still. Someone, somewhere, is laughing all the way to the plank bankS

67 Green Ink
Thursday 2 October

CBT it's called – Cognitive Behavioural Therapy. Means as little to me as it does to you, probably. Just an intimidatingly fancy name for talking-cure shrinkery, I reckon. But anyway, I've got 12 weeks of CBT ahead.

The room is fairly Spartan. Empty bookcases, just a computer. Rather different from the other shrink, C, whose bookshelves were heaving with erudite tomes and huge bottles of Moet. Since this is an Essex day, I go in to see the shrink, M, with my mother. Actually a huge relief, cos this part of Addenbrooke's was not built with wheelchair access in mind, so she has to walk ahead and open doors.

'What is CBT?' She asks M as we sit down. M has obviously been asked this before and starts drawing charts and diagrams. IN GREEN INK.

I don't know quite where my prejudice against green ink came from. I do remember V on *A Week in Politics* bemoaning his crapulous post from the 'green ink brigade'. Certainly I used to joke that green inkers were monomaniac nutters. But then I went to the Sindie, where I was sent a letter in green ink, diagrams and all. From Ian Brady. Protesting about Broadmoor. Green ink wasn't so funny anymore.

Pen Pal

68 Willpower
Friday 31 October

Ialways get up early, but there's good reason today, for it's November tomorrow, and I must smoke as many fags as I can while its still October.

Every year, I pack it all in for the winter; partly to avoid the cold and wet of outdoors, and partly to prove to myself that I still can. This year I'm being joined in my abstinence by 2 others: Too-Cool-for-School middle daughter and her even cooler boyfriend. So I must not fail. Crap!

 On the plus side, my tremor is so flipping dreadful these days that I drop fags all the time and endanger everyone with a Kings Cross style conflagration.
So expect me to be in a fouler mood than normal till February. Expect to see me taking snuff, or smoking one of those stupid fake fags. And congratulate me, admiring my groovy willpower. And hope for horrid weather.

69 Pee
Friday 14 November

A good day today. Certainly compared to yesterday which was effin' awful, with a bad fall on the rock-hard floor and wet myself and the bed at least five times.

Got an appointment with GP booked for this afternoon to discuss my peeing problems, so that involves taking a sample of piss in a test tube to the docs. Sounds easy, eh? Piss-easy? But no. For a start, the test tube is small, way smaller than my – ahem – you know....

There's balance, too. With my only working hand holding a test tube, I can't use it for its normal purpose – holding on to the loo. So I lean and nearly fall lots of times. But in the end, success. I have a test tube half filled with pee to take to the nice doctor, who will doubtless stick a bit of litmus paper in it and then throw it away (well I hope so!).

I'm better today anyway. So this appointment is not exactly vital in any case.

70 Milk
Tuesday 18 November

In many ways I'm one of the lucky ones. I love milk.

There are plenty of people – my Long-Suffering Wife for starters, who would rather taste a glass of piss than one of milk, but not me. Pizzaland does milk, and I usually choose it to go with my American Hot Milk, you see, is a lot thicker than water or wine, and not fizzy like beer or Coke, all of which make me cough and it goes everywhere and all over L-S W's new outfit

I must at this point make my excuse, feeble as it is. My dear friend L is an artistic genius. Particularly with concrete. And he gave me a lovely present the other day. A concrete ash tray. In 3 colours. Not to use it for 3 months would be rude, don't you think? So I did. A perfect, albeit utterly crap, excuse.

Tuesday 25 November

For the dying – me in this case – visitors are something of a cross to bear. Everyone wants to see and chat with the afflicted. They always come just as something unmissable – like Pointless – is about to start on TV. Oh well.

My friends, L & J had a better idea – they just posted cash for a curry. So, enough nastiness for today. It's Xmastime. Many people have commented that I am the most abusive and unpleasant person they have ever met. That just suggests that they haven't met my pal SoC, a master of the sideswipe.

But abuse has an unnecessarily bad reputation. Back in 1988 a referendum was held in Chile to decide Si or No to 8 more years of Pinochet. Had I worn a t-shirt with 'Pinochet is a murderer' emblazoned on it, I would have been beaten up and deported. So instead, for days I wore a silly hat with 'pin8 es feo'* written on it. No policeman stopped me: call a dictator an assassin and they know what to do – but call him ugly and they're flummoxed. So, abuse is cool and clever. So eff off.

*Pin8 (Pin-ocho) is a shortening for Pinochet, the phrase means 'Pinochet is ugly'

In leaner days, Santiago 1988

Charlie wrote the following for the National Library of Chile:

My girlfriend (now wife) Lucy Alexander and I arrived in Santiago in August 1988. It was an exciting time and we were privileged to witness it. Although Lucy had to return to university in September, I stayed throughout the *plebiscito* campaign, not flying back to England until the end of October.

The first pamphlet I kept was a 'Sí' leaflet, suggesting that, under the opposition, children would learn to count by adding bombs and AK47s. I thought it ludicrous, and worth keeping as a memento.

Then I attended a demonstration by the wives of disappeared men, outside the *Estadio National* [National Football Stadium]. Within minutes, the women had been arrested and the pamphlets seized by *carabineros* [Chilean police]. The fact that I had managed to grab a few put, it seemed to me, a duty on me to keep them. Their powerful question – '¿me olvidasté?'[Have you forgotten me?] – suggested to me that it would be an insult to throw the pamphlet away. And so the collection began.

Throughout the month of September, my collection grew. And it wasn't hard to find more. It seemed that almost every day would bring a new addition, whether it be a handmade 'No' from the children in *La Victoria* [the epicentre of opposition to Pinochet's dictatorship], or a folding pocket-sized attack on Ricardo Lagos [leading Socialist politician in the alliance that overthrew Pinochet, later president of Chile] from the 'Sí' campaign. Most of these pamphlets were picked up from the pedestrian streets of Santiago. Generally speaking, *Huérfanos* was a goldmine for 'Si' literature, while the *Paseo Ahumada* favoured the 'No'.

There were other notable advertisments, too. The pages of *La Epoca* and *El Mercurio* were a goldmine. In particular, one advert, purporting to be from the PS [Socialist Party], urging voters to '*anular tu vota*' looked suspiciously like a fraud.

On the day of the vote, my host, Dr Ricardo Badilla, was sent by the *Commando por el No* to *La Victoria* to oversee the collation of results from the count. The final two faxes from the collection are from that night. The first – sent while the TV results service was still off the air – gives the full official vote count by the *Comando por el No*. Within an hour or so, we received the second fax, informing us that the 'Sí' campaign had acknowledged defeat.

The 1988 plebiscite was my first introduction to politics, elections and journalism – and those three have underpinned my career ever since. In both newspapers and television, my fascination with politics and elections has remained undimmed, and my latest job will be to produce a world politics programme for TV.

Until now, my collection of pamphlets has been gathering dust on my shelf in England. It is a pleasure and a privilege to be able now to return to Chile and put the pamphlets where they belong – in the *Biblioteca Nacional*. They were written and printed for the people of Chile, and I salute the designers and authors who created them.

[Written in February 2006 on a visit to Chile.]

Friday 5 December

It's the lead story every night on Look East these days. That paedo cancer doc at Addenbrooke's with his cool cameras disguised as pens, like something you get free with Whizzer and Chips. But he rightly got caught, is going to jug, and now has a Criminal Record forever. But at least he knows about it. I, too, have a criminal record. AND I DIDNT KNOW!

About 10 years ago, some kind neighbours gave us five black sheep. Near neighbours, but ACROSS THE COUNTY BOUNDARY – IN SUFFOLK. The neighbours' vet came and checked them over, all fine.

Next thing we knew, a policeman turned up with one of those Inspector Morse tape recorders. He had a coffee and we discussed the lovely sheep and how that arse of a vet had blagged on us cos due to Bluetongue restrictions, it was technically illegal to move sheep over county boundaries. I said sorry, shook hands, he left. End of story.

Then, several years later, I had a full London day. BBC White City in the morning, meeting in Angel afternoon. It was a lovely day, so I decided to walk. The shortest route was over the Westway. Unfortunately, that is a motorway and walking isn't allowed. Cue Police Van, all flashing lights and woo woo noises.

I was bundled into the back where a plod sat with a snazzy laptop.
"Name, sir? Address, sir?" etc.
Then, "have you got a criminal record, sir?"
"No, of course not. What are you..?"
"As a matter of fact, sir, you have. For the illegal transportation of sheep."

They were very nice about it all, those cops. Even gave me a lift to Angel. And turned on their woo-woos. But still. How can you not know you've got a criminal record? And will someone be taking sneak photos of me in Addenbrooke's next week?

Illegal black immigrants from Suffolk seek asylum in Essex

Tuesday 9 December

My wife and my mother have both appealed to me to make this one more upbeat, jollier, than recent efforts. I'll try, but given that I have an appointment tomorrow with the urology clinic at Addenbrooke's for a new catheter, laughs may me a mite sparse. I relish a challenge though. Little Britain, that vastly-overrated comedy show, got laughs from the sight of someone pissing themself, so I will do likewise. Anything David Walliams can do – except swim, of course.

It was Auschwitz that really brought it home. As a naturally fun-loving family where better for an Easter break? So that was last year's jaunt. My bladder, already ropey from the ferry and the inter-rail, let me down big time. I usually describe my 'banding' symptom as akin to wearing wet trousers. It isn't. Wet trousers are horrid; banding just spooky. All the fun of Auschwitz spoiled!

I love Christmas; unlimited Brussels sprouts and Brandy Butter, Perry Como and Jona Lewie songs and Dick van Dyke movies and the always-on telly. My wife doesn't. Probably for similar reasons.

Tuesday 16 December

My kind friend H, who works at the Beeb, has sent me a stash of DVDs from the corporation library to keep me amused while I wait for this new catheter to kick in. (The first few days with it have been a bit horrid).

The DVDs span the very best and the very worst that the Beeb can offer. There's the Bronowski series on *The Ascent of Man*. On the other hand, we have *Weekend with Rod Liddle*, a programme which only ran to four episodes before it was killed off. It has never before been borrowed from the Beeb, but it is hugely instructive to those of us interested in TV current affairs. As I wrote in the *Sindie*[*] when it aired, 'The worst programme anywhere, ever, in the History of Time. You've simply got to see this before they kill it…' Not enough people believed me, and a week later, it was history, put out of licence-fee payers' misery.

It's bumper double issue time at Radio Times – confirmation of joyful festive TV. Not much on this year, so we watched *Elf* pre-recorded yesterday. Ever keen to see when I'd blub, Long-Suffering Wife turned round to watch my reaction.
Was seeing Zooey singing in the shower enough?
Will Ferrell's homemade decorations?
No, Santa's sleigh getting Christmas spirit did the trick and opened the floodgates.

With the stark title of this blog, I'll get back to the point. My 'more than one, fewer than five' prognosis of last year allows for quite a lot of leeway, so – at the risk of looking a ninny – I'll be a tad more specific in my predictions. I reckon this will be my last Xmas. As Wham!
didn't say.

Sunday 21 December

A bumper Christmas double issue for all our readers. Bad luck.

When DF and I flew off to Baku to interview the president of Azerbaijan, Aliyev, it was quite a big deal for both sides. Aliyev wanted to be seen as open, honest etc. I was equally determined that we should not be seen as walkover patsies, let him off the hook etc. So I wrote a 130-page brief for DF to plough through.

On the night before the interview there was a knock at my hotel door. It was one of Aliyev's flunkeys. A miserable arse with greasy hair and an ingratiating manner.
"I have here a list of questions which Sir David may NOT ask under any circumstances. These questions are off limits."
"Oh good. If you show me that list, I can guarantee 2 things. First, we will ask every one of those questions and secondly, we will ask WHY we weren't allowed to ask them."
"Harrumph". An intimidating notebook came out and scribbles made.
To be continued later…

The subject of writing everything down is particularly germane to the not-for-much-longer. Do you write THE LETTER to your partner/kids/whatever to be opened – ahem – after? If so, what should you say?

One of the benefits of a wheelchair existence is that, once your chair is packed in the hold, you can't move on a plane, and so you have hours to do with as you please. Like write THE LETTER. So I did one, en route to Johannesburg last year. But what to say? My pal H, who has herself died since, told me that there are just 4 things you have to say: thank you, I love you, I forgive you and I forget the 4th but I'm sure it was wise.

Baku cont.
The next day, DF and I went to the president's hideous chintzy palace. The flunkey was there and had a new method of intimidation: every time I spoke, everything I said, was written down, longhand, in the notebook.
The interview was good. DF asked all the right questions and Aliyev looked an arse. But the flunkey wanted more. He insisted on making copies of the tapes. I refused to let them out of my sight. So had to watch the copies being dumped [transferred] , all the while with ghastly flunkey taking copious notes.
Eventually, the tapes finished copying and flunkey went for a pee, LEAVING HIS NOTEBOOK.
"You've buggered up my day. So now I'm going to bugger up yours," I thought, as I scooped up my tapes – and his book

I have it still. Even though I can't write. It is one of my most prized possessions.
Moral: don't trust journalists. We are wankers

76 Creative tension (bumper New Year double issue)
Tuesday 30 December

Many people have, over the years, asked the same question. "How come a wanker like you ends up with DF, who loved what you hate, eg sport, cigars, celebs etc., and hated what you love, eg Bloody Mary, garlic, fags etc?" The answer is simple: Creative Tension.

Our tale begins in May 2005. As TV critic at the Sindie, I was asked to write a profile of a guy I had never met, but USING HIS STYLE OF CHEESY QUESTIONS.

It was fun to write, but I wasn't to know that I would be asked to work with DF within months. Lots of people in TV are advocates of Creative Tension, the conviction that if people fundamentally disagree or are put out of their comfort zone, magic will ensue. It's drivel, but never did me any harm.

And that's what happened at Jazeera. I will give full credit to David for this – he was much more forgiving than me. We just had to find a way of working. And we did.

The journalistic view of David Frost is usually less than kind. Revered over in the States, Frostie is less regarded in his homeland. The public takes him for granted, and journalists recoil from his sycophancy: the unctuous interview style is frowned upon by a chattering class, which prefers the Rottweiler style of Paxman, or the repartee of a Dimbleby. But nobody can deny that Frost gets the guests, and his passing from the Sunday morning slot, the last programme goes out this morning, will leave a hole. His replacement, Andrew Marr, will doubtless be a far cannier question-phraser. But will he get the guests, or will Breakfast with Marr become just another Sunday show for political anoraks?

What's the secret of your success?
In one view of the story, David Frost is just plain lucky. He happened to be in the right place at the right time, and that place was Cambridge's Footlights revue at the turn of the Sixties. Hot on the heels of the trail blazed by the Beyond the Fringe quartet, Frost didn't miss his golden opportunity. He began presenting TV shows while still an undergraduate, and made his mark almost immediately. That Was The Week That Was, TW3, made headlines even before it grabbed viewers. Frost fronted the show, which introduced the likes of Bernard Levin, Millicent Martin, John Bird and Eleanor Bron to an audience unused to irreverence and controversy. Frost's devastating profile of the then home secretary, Henry Brooke, ensured that the minister's reputation was tarnished for ever, while Frost's name was inextricably linked to the satire boom thereafter. The attention he garnered did not go down well with some of his peers: Peter Cook always claimed that his greatest regret in life was in saving Frost from drowning in a swimming pool. TW3 did not run for long: only just over a year, and Frost's Atlantic journeys began soon after. Leaving the rest of the team behind, Frost took TW3 to NBC in the US, and it proved a hit there, too.

I understand you're hosting a glittering party: Just how many wonderfully famous people will be there to pay homage?
With his name established on both sides of the Atlantic, Frost returned to the BBC with The Frost Report and The Frost Programme. Still in his mid-twenties, David had already managed to get his name in the programme title, and it was an honour he would never relinquish. However talented his co-presenters over the decades - Ronnie Barker and Ronnie Corbett, John Cleese, Esther Rantzen, Rory Bremner - there was never again to be any doubt about who was the star. Frost's relentless networking and hosting of famous parties has ensured that he maintains the reputation of the man with access. But it has also led to snobbery and envy, the accusation that the grammar school boy with the flat vowels is also a namedropper and a social climber. The gossip was fuelled when his first marriage, to Peter Sellers's widow Lynne Frederick, lasted barely a year. When he chose Lady Carina Fitzalan-Howard as his second bride a year later, few observers thought it would last. Twenty- three years later, their marriage remains.

Do you think that being a celebrated interviewer is sufficient recognition of the breadth of your talents?
Frost's transatlantic reputation reached new heights when in 1977 he persuaded the recently disgraced Richard Nixon to permit Frost's cameras in for a 28-hour session. The five programmes which emerged remain the most watched news interview in history. But TV stardom was not enough. Frost wanted to be a mogul, too. In 1967 he had been one of the founders of London Weekend Television, and one of the 'famous five' founders of TV-am in 1983. Even last year he was still at it, running for the BBC director-general's

job. But these attempts have usually ended in disappointment. Frost's LWT was criticised for promoting bland entertainment over more worthwhile programming. TV-am famously dissolved in acrimony, and Frost was passed over for DG. He does, of course, have that knighthood. And few who work on Frost's programmes are allowed to forget it. He's 'Sir David', and make-up artists and floor managers had better remember that. But for every snide whisper, there's a loyal and supportive colleague. Barney Jones, who has edited Breakfast with Frost for 12 years, thinks he knows why the professional hacks snipe: 'David doesn't have a background in journalism, he's never prepared a news bulletin and doesn't slave away over a terminal for hours on end checking the wires. But one of his skills as a broadcaster is encouraging people to talk and being at ease himself whether the camera is running or not. Just last week we had a schoolboy on the show, the star of Billy Elliot, and David was as comfortable talking to him as he was talking some months ago to George Bush.

I loved your last interview: will your next ones be even better?
Political interviewing remains his cornerstone. But his perceived closeness to John Major was to prove a stumbling block: it was when Major gave the broadcaster a knighthood in 1993 that the gossip about him being a 'patsy' really began. But this reputation lives on; it hasn't prevented him securing a contract to carry on doing interviews with big political, sporting and cultural names until 2008.

Do you prefer chintz or satin?
Frost's reputation for a fascination with style over substance was sealed when he began to front Through the Keyhole, a TV version of Hello! Magazine. Again, Frost confounded the critics. Through the Keyhole has run for 20 years, produced by Frost's own company, Paradine Productions, and is one of the few programmes to have successfully transferred from ITV to the Beeb's daytime schedules. Yet again, the glasses and blazer boy proved himself ahead of the game.

Is there a hidden side?
But, of course, there's another view. The give-'em-enough-rope position, which suggests that the most anodyne of questions can elicit the most revealing of answers. 'When the president does it, that means it's not illegal.' That's a great quote from Richard Nixon. Arguably the best he ever gave, encapsulating in a few short words the Nixon White House's view of Watergate. And Frost got it. You only get the quote if you get the guest. Yes, the argument runs, Frost may be fawning and cheesy. But he gets the right guests, and gives them the opportunity to hang themselves – or not. Tony Blair, no less, has often used Frost's programme as a friendly arena for announcing new initiatives, most famously when in 2000 he revealed plans for increased health spending, leading Gordon Brown to tell him privately "You've stolen my fucking budget".

Undeniably Breakfast with Frost has realised the aspiration of so many news outlets, setting the agenda for the week. Neither could anyone accuse Frost, 66, of being a slacker. He works hard, and is rarely distracted by illness: during one memorable live interview a couple of years ago, Frost suddenly developed a terrifying nosebleed. He carried on relentlessly, with only a disembodied floor-manager's hand encroaching in the shot to dab at the torrent. A Richard-and-Judy land, where only interviewers like Frost existed, might be a horror to contemplate. But so might one in which all interviewers see themselves as dogs to a guest's lamp-post there's surely a place for the smooth style alongside the rough. Breakfast with Marr has a tough act to follow.

2015

77 Two NHS tales from one day

Tuesday 6 January

I wrote at 2.00am to our kind MS nurse, M, telling her that 3 times in a day my new catheter had leaked and soaked everything, me included. Within hours I had spoken to the district nurse and have a new leg bag on. Fingers crossed. NHS crisis – what crisis?

But then I'm middle class, sober, white.

This evening a guy knocked on our door and introduced himself as Gilbert from South Africa. Said his leg was broken. One look confirmed it. Kind Climb-anything 13-year-old son took pity and invited him in. 999. The answerer tried instant down-the-line triage. Not helped by the fact that Gilbert was

a) drunk
b) verbose and
c) heavily accented in Zulu
d) suggesting that he had been hit and run – by a bicycle! (We get a lot of them here in Swotsville.)

So the verdict was maybe an ambulance; if we wait 2-3 hours! Gilbert needed A & E now, quite apart from the fact that he was cluttering our hallway and falling off his chair. So my kind Long-Suffering Wife drove him to Addenbrooke's. Climb-anything-son went too, clutching a sushi knife that I'd bought in Thailand last year, cos he'd recently watched a horror film in which a stranger asks for help then wipes out a whole family. Gilbert didn't look hungry, but you never know! They dropped Gilbert at A and E and raced home for supper. Gilbert is probably still in a queue.

78
Tuesday 13 January

They are a Scandi-noir import, rather like *The Bridge*. But now that I have to spend pretty much all day in bed, I must face my horror – I can't do duvets.

What is supposed to be flat, and always is on adverts for cheapo hotels on TV, when sexy girls have pillow fights, instead wraps itself like a cocoon round me. I can't move. Help!

The upshot is that I can't get my arms out to reach the TV control to turn over. That's my excuse for watching *Father Brown*, anyway.

79 Control
Sunday 18 January

Effin unfunny, this one. Beware!! Not a good loo read. Or after kippers for breakfast.

If The Stranglers are anything to go by there are 'No More'. But this time they're wrong – or were, at least. Cos my hero died last week. And perhaps in a way she would have wanted – starvation!

One of the most annoying things about this effing MS is the total loss of independent CONTROL over anything. I wholly rely on wheelchairs, bed controls, Long-Suffering Wife, TV remotes, carers, kids, specs, parents etc. to be in the right place at the right time. Otherwise I am stuffed. It's so demeaning. I seem to have few options. And then Debbie Purdy* came along.

I want to emphasise at this point that THIS IS NOT AN OPTION THAT I PLAN TO TAKE. But having it as a choice is such a relief. And it's not nice. It involves buying a one-way ticket to Switzerland, if you get me.

Debbie Purdy was in pretty much the same situation as me. If she were to go to Switzerland, she would need the help of her beloved husband, Omar. But it transpired that if Omar wheeled Debbie, even bought her a Swiss map, he'd be liable to prosecution for Assisting a suicide. So Debbie took it to court – right up to the Lords, and she won.

In the end, Debbie took another route. I assume that, like me, she had a 'living will' to prevent the insertion of tubes which would enable the force-feeding of a patient like a fois gras goose. So she starved herself to death. Good for you, Debbie. My hero.

DF + DP. RIPx2

*Charlie's article about Debbie Purdy is at the end of the book

81 The H word and Eighteen Years a Slavey
Thursday 22 January

Where?

My lovely GP, J, asked me whether I have any preference henceforward. Actually I don't. She is talking to the hospice about me going there. I probably will, but I doubt they'll let me smoke there. Crap!

As if dying wasn't a big downer anyway. Packing in the fags is worse. The hospice looked really nice the time I visited, but still… Why do people seem to care so much about WHERE they die? I don't give two hoots. I care THAT I'm a goner, not where.

Meanwhile, Long-Suffering Wife and I drove Slavey 18-year-old daughter to Heathrow for a flight to Chile. She's going to South America for 6 months. Following in L-SW's footsteps.

It was poignant; I may not see her again. And I don't want her rushing back and spoiling her once-in-a-lifetime trip on my account. On the other hand, wouldn't it be kinda spooky to be on holiday during your dad's funeral? Not my problem, thank goodness.

Monday 2 February

A rthur Rank. Swotsville

NAME Arthur Rank made gazillions in flour Rank-Hovis-MacDougall and movies (loincloth-wearing gong-beating muscleman hunk for whom I am frequently mistaken).

Legend (aka Wikipedia) has it that, as a devoted Methodist, Rank poured cash into medical works like this. Good for him. Better coming from Arthur than from his colleagues Clovis Hovis or Dougal MacDougall.

(Accurate sciency-sounding score to 1 decimal decimal place = 97.3%)

ROOMS   4 doubles 4 singles. all with En suite 90.9 %
CLEAN   very very. like Grandma Judy: 99.9 %
LOCATION   As with many hospices, AR House is tucked away out of sight. Consequently, the view from my window is inward: 77.1%
STAFF   Lovely. Not at all like witches = 100.0%
FOOD   Yummy, very decent = 86.7
ACCESS TO SNEAKY FAG PLACE EVEN UNDER SNOW WITH MANUAL WHEELCHAIR
TOTAL   98.4%

83 I am a number, but I'm free
Sunday 8 February

5pp0569761. The wristband I've got on has my name, date of birth and NHS number on it. Name misspelled of course. Why does everyone seem to think there's an H in my surname? I don't pronounce one, do I? I wore the wristband for the duration of my 5 days in the hospice, and haven't yet taken it off in case I need to go back in today (they are keeping my bed available, just in case). You're only supposed to go into hospice if you are reckoned to have 6 days or fewer left, so their keenness to see me again isn't reciprocated.

The snorey git who shared a room with me at first was even more insufferable after I'd gone. He even accused the nurses of getting into his bed! Chance-d be a fine thing, pal.

Anyway, back home now. Lovely supper with some friends yesterday, and kind wife and kids had made my room super-cosy. There was a plan to get me a tattoo (pug) today; great idea, but I'm not sure I'm up to it.

Back to Essex till Friday tomorrow.

85 Gabapentin
Friday 13 February

It's a powerful pill, this Gabapentin stuff. It's often prescribed for Parkinson's but it's not uncommon with this MS tremor too. But unlike Lily the Pink's medicinal compound, it has declining efficacy. And there are side-effects, not least in sending me to sleep.

The Delicate balance seems to have swung. As it seems to with pretty much anything, I'm so often faced with that choice – stick with something as it gets less and less effective, or pack it in altogether. I'm prescribed gazillions of the damn things – 9 a day, I think – and would love not to see them ever again. Plus, Look East had a story last week about how heroin junkies are taking up Gabapentin too. So stuff that. It tastes very nasty, too. And it keeps changing from one stupid name to another, depending on which arm of Big Pharma is making it. Pfizer presents Neurotonin today.

So, should I stop popping the pills? That's the dilemma. I get some kind of Cold Turkey if I go off em. So what do you suggest?

86 Pain
Saturday 21 February

It doesn't hurt, not much anyway. It's just an effin pest. My head nods as if I agree enthusiastically with whatever baloney has just been said – even though it's probably drivel. I never agree with anyone, so it's torture to give that impression.

Pain is, as a rule, rather painful and generally to be avoided. So it was with rather a shaming mix of emotions that I heard the news of that stem cell trial from my kind pal E this week (see no 13). Apparently, while I pulled out of the trial, one guy, T, stuck with it. I wanted it to work for him, or thought I did, but when I heard that it hasn't really worked, has left T in agony, then I was at least an eensy bit relieved.

Someday, someone is going to find a cure for MS. But I'll be long gone by then – and not in much pain.

Wednesday 25 February

It has sustained me and Long-Suffering Wife for ages. Call it arrogance if you will (and plenty of you do – bastards). I prefer to call it inventiveness, or cleverness, or somesuch. Sounds better, huh?

As I said ages ago (number 00 of these notes) this dying thing is really quite interesting.

Every day presents a new puzzle (how can I sign this letter with my unnatural right hand only? Can I transfer from this bed to that wheelchair? Can I type when I can't see? Etc) which we try to crack in a clever, outside-the-box way. And hitherto that has been enough.

But as we approach the – ahem – conclusion, the puzzles become both greater in number and harder to crack. I used to love quizzes: I got banned from enough pubs in the 80's for milking their quiz machines. But MS is not like Give Us A Break, more's the pity. If I cant read the subtitles on The Bridge or Wallander, there isn't a clever way round it. I'm just buggered. And just turning over to News 24 is of diminishing value.

What once was interesting is becoming boring. Like Spooks.

88 Flick
Tuesday 10 March

My pals P and P and M and J all drove off for a 'lads weekend' of movies, cigs, curry, beer and bridge in Berkshire. Luckily, P has a brother-in-law who has access to all the BAFTA-nominated films, so I never needed to pull my solitary offering out of my overnight bag. It was a movie I had been given as a freebie, but wasn't keen to watch: Frost/Nixon.

[An excerpt from Charlie's diary]
It's July 2006. The channel hasn't even go a name yet; Jazeera International? English? In a goodwill gesture, DF and I took a tour of studios in Doha, KL and Washington.

The 'hubs' were a shambles of dangling wires and cardboard boxes. DF loved it. But that's not our subject for today. It's the flight. As is his way, DF was in First Class, seat A1. As is mine, I was in Stowaway Class with caterwauling babies and excess luggage in shitville at the back.

DF toddled down the aisle to me with a copy of a new play from Peter Morgan, and asked me to read it and pass on comments. He then toddled back, and I settled down to read.

A few minutes later, a stewardess rushed out of first class. 'Is there a medical doctor on the plane?' she pleaded. My immediate thought was 'oh crap. My presenter's copped it.' But I carried on reading and didn't go up to First till I'd finished. It turned out that the alarm was nothing to do with DF. He was sitting in one of those cubicle-type seats, sipping a glass of his usual ultra-sweet white.
I handed back the play.
'What did you think?'
'Do you want my honest opinion?'
'Go on.'
'You don't come out of it very well. You look like a twit, frankly. A total lightweight. It looks like your only interest is in getting the interview, and it's only the determination of your team which forces you to ask the right questions.'
'Oh. I thought that when I first read it. But John Birt said it was OK.'
'That's hardly surprising. John Birt comes out of it all right.' Then it was back to economy for the remainder of the flight.

Frost/Nixon was a smash hit of a play, and was shortlisted for hatfuls of Oscars when the film of it came out. Unusually, it seemed that I had been wrong to diss it. But I wasn't gonna watch it for fun. The dvd stayed in my overnight bag.

Jazeera Washington 2006

Thursday 12 March

Not moving – apart from this demented nodding – is pretty easy for me. So it was fairly simple for me to stay still when L, a book group friend of Long-suffering Wife, offered to capture me in charcoal

It does look like me. It also looks like Patrick Swayze.

And nobody has ever accused me of that before. And even though I can't see a flipping thing with this tremor, I can appreciate the genius of L.

Dude, by Lucy Threlfall

Tuesday 17 March

A pologies folks. This piece covers NEITHER of my two favourite topics viz

A) me, or
B) dying
But it does cover the health service.

Our Too-cool-for-school middle daughter was born with what in technical jargon is known as 'clicky hips'. It meant that she spent much of her early years in ghastly girdles or cumbersome plaster casts, and had jazillions of operations done by a doctor who looked creepily like The Demon Headmaster.

Anyway, we thought all that was behind us. Wrong! Great Ormond Street Hospital (GOSH) decided that she needs another op this Friday, which set Long-Suffering Wife into a frenzy of organisation, arranging in-law visits, my carers, people for Climb-anything son to stay with and for the school to allow our daughter's GCSE timetable to fit in.

But then GOSH suddenly decided to re-re-arrange things, telling L-S W that Friday was off. Cue wifely frenzy again. And then, prompted by wifely panic and GP disgust, GOSH have changed their minds AGAIN. Back on for tomorrow! Re-re-re-arrrangements.

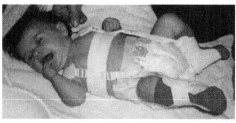

Early 1999 or so

Thursday 19 March

Remember that EDDS scale I wrote about earlier? It was that kinda useful disability list which had healthy at 0 and dead at 10. it was 9.5 which I really dread, bedbound and incommunicado. I'm heading that way – nobody, not even my lovely Long-Suffering Wife, can understand a word. Which is spooky, frankly. The words seem perfectly understandable to me… What sort of cretin doesn't get it? But it seems that everyone is that sort, and this typing, slow and erratic as it is, may be my only way of being understood. (It's the stupid predictive text that I hate the most)

While I'm at it, and at the risk of boring some of you, I should put down some requests for, ahem, after. I don't like Gosfield, much much prefer Colne Engaine*. prefer cremation, with ashes split 50/50.

My L-S W gets half, which goes to Inverkirkaig bay. My wonderful parents get half. If possible, that should go to the dog graveyard near Knights with 'and Charlie Courtauld' after 'Here lies Spot' or whatever on the headstone.

*Essex village churches. Gosfield is where many Essex Courtaulds are buried. Colne Engaine is where Charlie grew up and lived from 2000-2013.

92 Richard III
Monday 23 March

The last one was in some ways the saddest of these pieces. If, as I had expected, I become incomprehensible – am unable to speak or whatever – then I, you, might have assumed that I had become something of a simpleton.

I am plagued just now by this cretinous non-stop nodding which makes my neck hurt, but worse; it gives the deceptive illusion that I agree with you. I don't. You are talking drivel, however much I seem to concur. I'm not pitiable; not even I pity me. Believe me, I'm negative and nasty. I don't give a fig about the non-eclipse or Richard the third.[*]

Modern technology – this iPad for example – gives me an extended articulacy. Of course I welcome that, but it's not all good news. I can't move, or see. Shouldn't I just accept that and stop annoying people?

[*] Richard III, whose skeleton was found under Leicester car park, was reinterred in Leicester Cathedral on 26 March 2015.

93 Not dying...
Friday 27 March

It must be fairly galling to get flown out somewhere rather cool and have absolutely zip to say of any interest during your interminable 2-way interviews with rolling news. That's how it must have seemed to News 24's Tim Wilcox* this week, until, kerching! it looked like the co-pilot might have crashed on purpose. Suddenly there seemed to be some sort of point for Tim to freeze his hairdo on that stupid hill.

So it is for me. When I started writing this nonsense, nearly 2 years ago, I could see, move, talk. Now I can't do any of them. But the biggie is still to come. Like Tim Wilcox freezing up that French Mountain, I'm stuck. Move it, Andreas.

I have been accused before of having some kind of death wish. I don't. But I do think I'm effing useless just now. But – and it's a question I must ask: what if I don't die? Will I have run out of things to say – look a complete twit???

Tim Wilcox without even a spare shirt.

*Tim Wilcox was the BBC reporter sent to cover Germanwings plane crash in the French Alps on Wednesday 25 March 2014

Friday 10 April 2015

My 2 fave healthcare professionals visited together and delivered the bad news: "You are gonna live. You are fit and healthy. Expect 2 more years at least"

Sounds good, no? No. Why not, arse?

Just imagine 2 years of this:

I can't see except blurry.

I can't hear a sodding thing with my left ear. It's got tinnitus too. Really boring tinnitus.

I can't move. As you may have noticed, I can actually type. Just. One finger, wrong hand.

I can't talk and be understood.

I dribble like one of those disgusting dogs. Even on my fag so I can't light it. I nod all the flipping time.

All of the above gets worse every day. It won't get any better. Bugger.

I am not suggesting that all this drivel makes me want to buy a one-way ticket to Switzerland. I won't. This is all too interesting for that. But it is nasty.

In sentences like 'the natives are restive', why is 'restive' a synonym for 'restless'? Shouldn't they be antonyms?

95 Hallucinations
Tuesday 28 April

I now have 2 super carers, Amber and Gina who come every morning at 7 to shower me and get me dressed for the day.

I was nevertheless surprised to see Amber on Monday because Gina had told me that poor Amber was going to prison this week, caught trying to nick a Cadburys Flake from Tesco. I remembered the conversation clearly. Only it never happened. I made it up. Bum. I rather fancied that flake.

Then, last night, I was certain that my father and was sleeping next to me in my bed. But I could tell it was a hallucination. No snoring for starters.

So what is the point? Why do I keep making things up? And why is it taking me ages to write this shitty piece? Firstly, I look it up on Wikipedia, but it doesn't seem very relevant. These hallucinations aren't scary, not at all. They're not even that interesting. I don't like flake that much.

And it's this non-stop nodding which I blame for my slowness. I can't flipping see the screen right in front of me. Not a hallucination. Wish it was.

96 My election
Monday 4 May

Bored of all those manifestoes? Don't be. Elections are fab. I obviously have quite a strong personal interest in this election. David Cameron was in my year at Eton and ed Miliband used to work with me on awip [*A Week in Politics*], so I can at least give a considered answer to the most obvious question. (Ed, by a mile)

But 2015 is not the one that I think of as 'my election'. That was the otherwise entirely forgettable poll of 2001. Blair v Hague's silly hat, and an entirely predictable country-mile win for Tony. I had always had 2 ambitions: to be a newspaper leader-writer during an election, and to work on a bbc all-night vote-fest with David Dimbleby. In 2001, I did both.

Back in those days, I was pretty recently diagnosed, so had a lot more stamina than now. Kind license-payers (thank you so much) put us up in the Hilton for 3 hours. Then off to the Sindie in time for morning conference with Janet. Other than needing to touch the walls of the bbc as I walked along, it was no big MS deal.

97 Tats amazing
Friday 5 May

There is something very spookily accurate about class. Attitudes to tattoos particularly. Being ridiculously snooty, I think tattoos are hilarious. Being comparatively common, my Long-Suffering Wife and my pal SoC hate tattoos.

So I had a pug engraved on my arm. And my Too-Cool-For-School daughter had my initials on her wrist. (By the way, she gave her wheelchair back to GOSH last week, and began her GCSEs today).

Our eldest, Slavey 18-year-old, is in Colombia now, and Climb-anything 14-year-old son is starting his new job this afternoon.

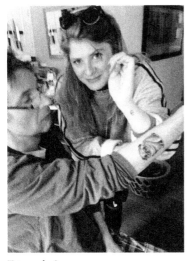

Tats cool x2

Wednesday 27 May

Yogurt, cheesecake, rice pudding, rhubarb. Puddings to you maybe, starters to Nick Soames maybe. But mains for me. They are pretty much all I can eat nowadays.

Given anything else, i cough, splutter and generally both disgust and frighten everyone around. Even salad: particularly salad, is a disaster (there have to be SOME compensations for this bastard disease).

So I am both startlingly easy and startlingly boring to feed. Yesterday my Long-Suffering Wife tried to pep things up by eschewing Ambrosia and making rice pudding herself. The rice was from the back of the larder somewhere. Mistake.

Given heaps of sugar and nutmeg, it tasted fine. But the consistency? It reminded me of something. Something from years ago. What was it? Ah, even with my dreadful memory, I won't forget that unique texture.

Copydex. I must have been about 8 when I gave up eating the White Stuff, convinced by some prep schoolmaster that Copydex was for glueing, not eating. But here it was again. Yum.

99 Fifa fo fum
Friday 29 May

It would be deeply unfair, simplistic and petty if I were to hope for a Blatter* victory in today's Fifa election, based solely on the fact that Greg Dyke wants him to lose. Tough.
Go President Sepp.

This permanent nodding and dribbling I now have, meant I was zero fun at the hospice yesterday (whereas I'm normally the life and soul, full of larks etc.) and wouldn't dream of dissing most of my fellow hospicers as malingerers. Tough again. You seem suspiciously well to me, merrily gobbling your chicken pie.

Then I have to apologise to you lot. I can't really type anymore with my effing head wibbling all the time – and with my eyesight a goner, it's too flipping hard. The fact that I don't write more stuff doesn't immediately mean I must be dead – only that I'm as lazy as you always thought. Tough.

* Blatter won the election but resigned shortly afterwards because of the FIFA corruption scandal

115

There's some good news: I didn't go to the hospice at all last week. Less good: that's because I was in hospital, surrounded by fatso boozers.

It all began on Tuesday. My lovely cousin, D, came down from Scotland for a visit. So I took her and our pooch for a long walk through the sights of Swotsville – by the river, Midsummer Common, Magdalene bridge, Eat coffee shop, Maplins, Parkers Piece, Tesco etc. It was great.

So proud was I, that I decided, the very next day, to do it again. Alone. Mistake.

It was pretty hot on Wednesday. Too bloody hot. I hate hot. It makes me flake out spectacularly. So it did. An ambulance was called, I was bundled in, and Addenbrooke's beckoned.

There is no MS ward, so I was put in the closest alternative – the Liver ward, with bed upon bed of aggressive yellow men in boxers, huge bellies and moobs on display. Their love of vodka and cake was all too visible.

My temperature went through the roof and I was totally out of it. Consequently, I was zero fun to visit. Too-cool-for-school daughter came, but I didn't notice her because I was asleep. Not, that is, until she crept back for the sunglasses she had left on my table. 'Get me my pills, bitch!' One man called to her, while I, noticing her at last, snapped 'don't steal my glasses!' Understandably, she fled.

There was loads of choice for food. Between inedible and filthy. The government were doubtless sensible to insist on food choice. They forgot to insist on quality.

101 Rules 1
Friday 3 July

You may have noticed – particularly those of you who get this drivel on email and are too lazy to go to charliecourtauld.tumblr.com – that, by useless counting, we are now into treble figures of these diatribes. But it occurs to me that I have not yet been explicit about the principles which underlie all of this. So, before I go, here are a few simple rules to bear in mind for broadcast journalists:

1. Producers are clever
2. Presenters are stupid, overpaid clothes horses etc. reading this as I write, my Long-Suffering Wife makes 2 valid objections
A) I was one of the worst and shittest ever presenters on the occasion when my presenter didn't show up.
B) One of our best friends is a very clever presenter. But there are exceptions to every rule.
3. Read the Economist, listen to the World Tonight and watch Channel 4 News
4. The BBC is good and wise and clever (except the National Lottery draw). But it is run like a potato.
5. TV is better than radio. Just a prejudice. But it pisses some people off, hilariously.

103 Shamblestalkathonis
Tuesday 14 July

Greece something of a nightmare today*. No Emergency Liquidity for them, and a finance minister with a name like Sack-the-lot-of-them-os. He did manage to talk to Christine Lagarde. For 17 hours!!

They should come to me. I got oodles of Emergency Liquid to spare today, drool, tears etc. I can't even light a fag cos the bloody thing is sopping and unusable by the time my lighter is lit. Pooh.

To Heathrow to collect Slavey 19-year-old daughter off the plane after 6 months travelling round South America for a gap year thingy. We drove with me in my wheelchair in the boot. Advantage: I don't have to move. Disadvantage: nobody can hear me. And with unbelievably rude Wife driving, that's a tragic loss, believe you me.

Now Slavey. Welcome home etc. Iced coffee please.

*Anti-austerity protesters had clashed with police following the Greek parliament's agreement to meet its creditors' demands

Saturday 25 July

And I've got one, two, three, four, five, senses working overtime…. When XTC sang about senses, insufficient attention was given to senses flagging. I can hear nowadays, but seeing, smelling, touching and tasting are gone. bum!

Do not be fooled into assuming that I must be able to see to type. In a sense, yes – but with font set at ginormous and with limited (zero) opportunity to retype.

We just went out to the Swotsville Botanic Gardens where there is a plant flowering which stinks and is only out for one day in a century, apparently. I could neither smell nor see.

All of which means that this piece is flipping short. Tough. Which leaves me with one, two er. Two-and a half. Umm…

With Daisy (Slavey) in the Cambridge Botanic Gardens

105 Rules 2
Friday 31 July

Here's another list of counterintuitive dross which should inform anyone who would like to be a current affairs/news producer. You should have gleaned them from earlier stuff anyway. But this is easier...

An important note. Please do not follow my advice, it will not get you a job. On the contrary. The last time I had a job interview at the BBC, circumstances could not have been better – I left my wheelchair AND the interviewer was a good friend AND the job was piss easy. I still didn't get employed!

A. Wikipedia is usually reliable, speedy and correct. Anyone who tells you to avoid are nitwits. To test this theory, David Dimbleby and I once changed HIS entry, putting in some whopper about a prison term, to see how long it would last. About 45 minutes.

B. Tabloids are tosh. In TV newsrooms it is often considered smart or clever to read the tabloids, particularly the Mail. Crap. Better the Beano, frankly. Any dunderhead reading the Mail should be avoided.

C. Lord Sewel* is wonderful. Probs.

D. Talkback is bloody fantastic. Ok, I looked a total arse when my presenter unexpectedly didn't turn up, but I did still manage a ten minute interview with Ian McEwan having never read a word. My secret? Talkback with Kate Newman, who had.

E. Think Again, Jeremy. Always remember who you are working for. Forget everything else. At the Sindie, I wrote harsh review of a TV prog fronted by Jeremy Vine. The next week, I got an email. "I thought we were friends". My three words in reply were also harsh. But fair.

*On 28 July 2014 Lord Sewel resigned from the House of Lords after being filmed allegedly taking drugs with prostitutes.

106 Scooby snack

Monday 17 August

Which of the Scooby Doo girls is sexiest? You are obviously supposed to prefer Daphne, with her long curly blonde locks. Not me. She's a frizzy haired nitwit, I reckon. Much better – despite a stupid name – is Velma, who is both clever and straight haired. She probably smokes too. Far away the coolest of the meddlesome kids.

So, what would Velma do in these circumstances? Nobody – not even my Long-Suffering Wife can understand a word I say, and I know that I would have booked a one-way to Switzerland by now, if I had known. But I didn't and I shan't. Not yet, anyway.

Because one of the spookiest things is how one can get used to pretty much anything. Give yourself a few days and you'll adapt to the lack of speech, wheelchair, tremor, dribbling, whatever.

107 – Shrinkanomics
Thursday 21 August

Last week, my Long-Suffering Wife, plus 3 kids, took a boating holiday. I stayed behind with the mutt and we went to Essex.

When family returned, showering me with cartons of gifts[1], they were full of tales of how unaffected Greece was by austerity etc. I hadn't even been outside Gods Own County, but I could prove them wrong, and I was holding the proof.

Shrink wrapping. With one working hand, plus teeth, I can usually open a pack. But then I came across a new phenomenon – AUSTERITY SHRINK WRAPPING, no wasted plastic. With no flap on the cellophane to grab with my teeth, it takes ages – sometimes an hour or more – to get my fag. Which leads me to this conclusion; how rich a country is, is related to the tightness of its shrink wrap.

Odd and revealing connections like that have always been a joy. Indeed, the BEST PROGRAMME IDEA I EVER HAD was one such. Cast your mind back to the ghastly battling Boers I had to deal with in South Africa. I needed some sort of wheeze to distract the researcher while I cracked skulls. So I emailed her:

DEAR LISA

As a global south freakonomics[2] comparitor, you could get Jaz bureaux in say 3 continents to get some numbers for you, In, say, Manila, Bangkok, Joburg, Nairobi, Rio, Mexico, how much do the following cost?

1. A gram of Cocaine
2. An assassination
3. A prostitute
Prob the bureaux won't help. But I would watch!
Nothing came of it, chiz.

[1] aka Cigarettes
[2] Charlie loved the book 'Freakonomics: A Rogue Economist Explores the Hidden Side of Everything' by Steven Levit and Stephen Dubner, which has been called a melding of pop culture with economics.

Tuesday 25 August

Everything has been very decent of late. Monday to Wednesday in Essex. Back home otherwise. Hurrah! Surely it can be repeated ad infinitum, no? No. Can't talk, can't see. For years, hooking up with Long-Suffering Wife to make a strong team has made us impregnable. Now we're stuffed.

It's not very surprising that the Beeb would like to replicate the success of Springwatch. So they have spent a bleeding fortune to bring us the underwater thrill of Big Blue Live. What a waste of money! No Chris Packham, no Kate Humble, no sticklebacks to watch.

Because a big part of the greatness of Springwatch is its cheapness. And a big part of beating this MS is that I can chat things through. Taking my speech is like taking Chris and Kate; understandable but cretinous.

109 Hospice
Thursday 3 September

Hospice day. Hence not a lot occurring. I can't talk anyway, and I'm a bloody nuisance at the best of times, so I rather spoil the 'blether' – the group discussion session. I seem to put unwelcome questions into the mix. Today I submitted a tricky one about Dignitas, but we concentrated on Britain's shameful treatment of asylum seekers.

Then lunch – which is, for me, a mouléed mixture. Today's pink gruel was allegedly sausage and mash with cauliflower. Yum – but why is it QUITE so pink after after a mouli? Were the 'sausages' really Aldi Frankfurters?

Outside for fags next. On my own which suits a curmudgeon like me perfectly. I don't have to talk. I am, of course, far and away the youngest (by about thirty years) who goes to day therapy at the hospice plus I'm the only bloke at the moment. Enough for anyone to light up.

110 Brothers
Sunday 13 September

The Brothers are in Brighton, I see. Brings it all back. Even to an arse with no memory. It used to be something of a doss, an easy-peasy bit of summer money for old rope for those of us who love making live TV. The trucks, the cables, the bubble soundproof studio, blah blah. Nice person to present, e.g. Francine Stock and Jackie Ashley, zero viewers. What can go wrong?

Plenty…

Before the time of News 24, live stuff on the Beeb was restricted to those of us in a truck in Brighton, and guests lined up to witter on about Trades Unions and resolutions and suchlike bollocks. I loved it.

Tuesday afternoon. Prime Minister is coming to speak. So the only real concern is that my presenter, Jackie, might have to interview her rather dreary and self-important husband, the BBC political editor, Andrew Marr.

As we went on air, a spooky story was on PA wires. A LIGHT aircraft (drunk pilot??!) had bumped into the World Trade Centre. As we went off air, both towers were down, Tony Blair had changed his speech (some shite about a kaleidoscope) and coverage was cancelled.

Everyone remembers where they were on September 11th 2001. I was down in some effing OB truck under the Brighton conference centre, trying to persuade some BALPA [British Airline Pilots Association] rep to talk about why all our flights were being cancelled.

111 Priorities
Saturday 19 September

It's kind of sad, kind of predictable. Corbyn has got his priorities all wrong. Republicanism or re-nationalisation or PMQ reform – all decent ideas which merit a place on any Labour leader's to-do list. About number 978 (8th term, maybe). The fact that Corbyn is already onto this stuff in week 2 bodes ill.

I can sympathise. I, too, have spooky priorities. As I write, my Long-Suffering Wife is driving our lovely Slavey daughter for her first day at Manchester University. So what the hell???

The answer is, of course, that I'm desperately doing it while I can. I'm flagging, frankly and losing all the clever gizmos I can to get this down. I don't think that there will ever be a number 112.

111.1 Corbyn
Wednesday 30 September

Sorry to bang on again, but I couldn't resist.

Just as everyone is trashing Jeremy Corbyn's rubbishy speech, the time has come for one of those counterintuitive counterblasts, i.e. what supercanny intervention.

1. Jeremy's enemy was not Dave C…the upcoming referendum on Europe means the Tories are going to be tearing themselves apart with no need of any encouragement from Labour. Anyway, without the likes of Tony Benn, Bryan Gould or Peter Shore, leftist anti-Europeanism is suddenly out of favour. (Actually, I rather liked that one).

2…it's Nicola S
Like some nightmare of Emily's List, the sharp suited and shoulder padded Miss Pastel-shade S and her SNP, have overrun former Labour territory

Now, by demonstrating that a rumpled suit and a messy beard can be just as compelling, we can expect the red Clyde to fall back into Labour's domain.

111.2 Panic
Friday 9 October

If there's one flipping annoying thing about all this. More irritating than piers Morgan, more ubiquitous than Huw Edwards, it's this: the panic attack.

Of course, it sounds a bit wimpy, feeble, ME-ey, etc etc to bang on about panic attacks.

But it's flipping debilitating and has been going on for yonks. Rob and the Thai trip? His Buddhist guru, Amani, was focussed on taking my mind off immediate worries about LSW and the kids, and, ahem, after. Now, at the hospice, we are trying to find something to listen to but unfortunately I smashed the relaxation CDs they gave me under my wheelchair while in a panic this morning. Bum!

111.4 A domestic
Thursday 15 October

Well, l suppose it had to happen. After 21 years of wedded bliss, LSW and I have come to an impasse, a profound disagreement.

I have, along with my lovely GP, written one of those 'living wills', written in rather naff terms, suggesting that neither in Cambridge nor Essex should I have anything to do with resuscitation or antibiotics. So there.

This will thing was written weeks ago and we have never had a problem with it. Until now.

This week, I reckon I got a UTI (Wikipedia for those not in TV). Following my rules and loathe to embarrass myself at the first hurdle, I stoutly refused medics. L-SW was appalled.

We were both right! A UTI is very painful, debilitating – but it doesn't kill you. To my mind, that means I should just grin and bear it (after all, I am a British boy), to L-SW's mind, I should just take the pills.

115 Roo
Wednesday 21 October

Kids love them. Even me, back in the day, thought them funny. But I don't like hiccups now. These days, a hic presages a significant downer.

Another thing, of course, which kids think tremendously funny is in getting grown-ups to believe whoppers and to act on them.

Last year, I was staying at a friend's house when my slumbers were interrupted by his granddaughter bouncing on my bed.

'Charlie, Charlie come quick. There's a kangaroo in the garden!'

No, there isn't! Do your geography.

'There is, there is. Come quick.'

Getting from bed to wheelchair to outside is not at all simple or quick.

It took about 10 minutes and plenty of pain.

'Charlie Charlie quick. A kangaroo!'

Crap. Now where?

Over there.

Blimey.

Monday 26 October

At the risk of repeating something which I suspect I have said before, I hate GMT. It is loved predominantly by scots, allegedly, to ensure that their school kids don't have to walk to school in the dangerous dark. So, the solution must be to permit them to have different time than England. That's why I supported a 'yes' in the scotch referendum.

But, I hear you object, doesn't Greenwich actually own the time, Harrison clocks, $0°$ longitude etc etc. It so happens that I know quite a bit about all this because I produced the Millennium Dome on New Year's Eve 1999.

At the time it was a groovy wheeze. To finish my TV career (I went to the Sindie a day later) working with my pal DD in Greenwich while Y2K* destroyed everything; what could go wrong?

The non-event of the 'river of fire', the Queen's rubbishy Auld Lang Syne….they were quite fun. But the crapulous Beeb pissed about with a rather cool 12 minute sunsets script which DD and I worked hard on for aeons

*The Millennium Bug that caused an unknown number of computers to fail as the clocks rolled over in 2000.

117 Fin
Thursday 5 November

From now on, do not believe a word I say. Not that you ever did, if you have any sense. But this is different. I don't just talk bollocks. I think bollocks too.

Whenever I'm asked why I write this weekly guff, my stock response is that it was a bet I had with Sue Douglas*. True, but incomplete. I know from 00 on that this disease has been pain-free. Hence, I know that this agony in my legs must be new.

Similarly, I know from previous blogs that I would normally discuss all this with L-S W. Again, I have no memory; relying on this blog. But I spent the last few days in lovely Essex, so no time to chat. Had a super break with a pug in Welsh Wales last week too. So, no chats with L_S W then either.

So, as we approach the – ahem – point of this blog, I need to make some things clear
I am not dying. Not very soon anyway
I am in awful pain. I've got a terrible tremor too,
My head shakes so much that I can't see.

*see no.29

Saturday 21 November

Women, they say, are good at multi-tasking. In my limited experience, they are spectacularly bad at it. This week, L-S W is on holiday, because her Millie Tant tendencies have necessitated her going away for a while.

This leaves me to go to Essex for the duration. As I've said before, Essex is lovely, but does involve a lot of *Bargain Hunt*, *NCIS* and *Murder She Wrote*.

To travel between the two locations, home and Essex, requires plenty of multi-tasking: careful packing up of all my medicines (inc. fags) and equipment; loading me and lots of clobber into our huge, specially-adapted vehicle; my mother driving here in our little red car and swapping into afore-mentioned disabled car; swapping parking spaces and permits; remembering the dog, and chargers for both kinds of Apple products and the wheelchair – and we're off. Not forgetting to flick a V sign at Suffolk as we zoom along the hideous Haverhill by-pass (where Too-cool-for-school middle daughter is learning to negotiate roundabouts).

So are women good at multi-tasking? Ask me after this week.

119 Schengen
November 25th

Amid all this Marseillaise-singing and air-striking Syria blether, nobody has pointed out the massive advantage of the Schengen system: sneaking small children with expired passports round Europe with zero passport checks.

The year before last, we all decided to go inter-railing across the continent. Too late, I spotted a flaw, – climb anything son's passport had run out.

What to do? Simmples.

I would love to is tell you how he did it.

But I'd have to kill you first.

Once we were inside Schengen, Europe was open. Holland, Germany, Poland, Czech Republic, France, Belgium and back to Holland. It was only when we were about to leave that the passport glitch was discovered. But what could they do? Deport us? That is what we wanted anyway.

Guilty as charged

Charlie dictated these last two blog entries

Saturday 5 December

Woodlands residential care home. Swotsville.

Bugger. I can't read or write anymore. This piece, for example, is written in a ginormous font so that I can see.

The staff here are kind if thick, all speaking their native (mostly Serbo-Croat) tongue. The idea is to stay here perhaps only until after Christmas, while L-S W finds a new care agency for me at home. But most of the time I think that I belong in a place like this, surrounded by demented old ladies who keep asking 'When is the concert tonight?' and mistake L-S W for staff and Too-Cool-For-School middle daughter for another patient.

You can't even smoke in your room, so I have to take the lift downstairs to go outside for a fag, which means that I had only two fags yesterday and two the day before.

Despite this, I think the more time I spend here, the more I belong here. When is the concert tonight?

2016

Saturday 2 January 2

At the hospice, but not for the – ahem – last time. This is all part of a cunning plot by Mary to minimise time spent in that shithole of a care home.

Actually, L-SW and I have our anniversary on New Year's Eve. It is 30 years since our first kiss. All those years ago, I held a party and we watched Diva, which, at that time, seemed to be on telly rather often.

For New Year's Eve I was allowed out by the hospice and, along with Climb-Anything Son, we watched Jools Holland and some rather dreary fireworks heralding in something I thought I would never see – 2016.

For New Year's Day we drove to Southwold which, despite being in Suffolk, is rather nice. Climb-Anything Son's girlfriend, who is, if anything more adventurous than he, came with us to do the traditional swim in the sea. Our family of five was supplemented by a sixth brave adventurer.

The howling gale and frightening waves didn't seem to put any of those idiots of – they simply ran into the freezing water while I, being sensible, treated myself to my first fag of the year.

122 Good bye Charlie
26 January

Charlie died at 7.30 am today. He was lying in bed surrounded by the children and me. He had a bladder infection last week that he couldn't shake off. So, contrary to what he wrote recently, bladder infections can kill you. He was incredibly brave and we miss him terribly already.

Charlie first wrote about his MS in a column in *The Independent on Sunday*, where he was working at the time. He started just a few weeks after he was diagnosed, on Wednesday 29 November 2000.

I would like to thank *The Independent* for their kind permission to reprint the following articles. Charlie loved his time at the paper and was very proud of all the work he did there.

My friend said I was imagining it. Unfortunately, I wasn't.

24 December 2000

"I know what you've got. It begins with H and ends with A." It was an understandable assessment from my friend. Hypochondria has long been virulent in my family, not least in me. Every headache, every twinge has been the precursor of something horrible – and then turned out to be nothing. My notes at the doctor's spill from three of those brown envelopes. So what was I so fussed about?

Have you ever been swimming with trousers on? I once had to as part of a life-saving course at school. It's no fun – trousers are nigh impossible to swim in, and when you get out of the pool, having rescued your drowning brick/plastic dummy/ fellow pupil, they're pretty hard to walk in too. So it was rather a surprise to wake up one morning in September to discover that I was wearing soaking trousers. It was an even greater surprise – bleary-eyed as I was at that time of the morning – to learn that I wasn't.

You see, I could feel the dripping garments with all their tightness and heaviness weighing me down, but I just couldn't see them. I hopped out of bed. As usual, just a T-shirt on. When I padded around, I could hardly feel my feet. Aled Jones may enjoy walking in the air, but I didn't.

Perhaps a doctor could help – but since we were on holiday in Spain, I wasn't going to rush to a clinic there and then. My Spanish isn't good enough: I can just about manage "nail", but "pins and needles" is well beyond me. Best to wait for a week until we got home – the trousers would surely have gone by then. Anyway, the sensation wasn't entirely unwelcome: one of the results was that I could now sleep with my feet touching each other, something I've always hated. I invariably keep Lucy awake as I thrash around in bed, trying to get comfortable. Now, none of that. It was into bed and straight to sleep. So, let it go, I thought. It'll pass before we get home.

It didn't, of course. It got worse. Now I had a big purple bruise on my foot where I'd stepped on one of my daughters' plastic fishing rods. But I couldn't even feel that.

So, the doctor's surgery. With autumn approaching, the waiting room was heaving with coughers and snifflers. Being new to the area, I hadn't met my GP before. After a series of pricks and brushes, straight-line walking and reflex tests, he tut-tutted and referred me on to a neurologist, Giles, in Colchester. Despite sporting that compulsory doctor's neckwear, the bow tie (which one might have hoped had gone out of fashion after Harold Shipman), Giles was a friendly bloke – but seemed to agree with my friend's diagnosis. "Go away for a month. A viral inflammation of the brain. It'll probably disappear. Come back in four weeks if it hasn't."

So I went away, rather shamefaced, and waited for the symptoms to pass. And, hey presto, they did. But new ones came instead. The wet trousers were off, but now I kept bumping into things. Walls, bollards, cars, lift doors. If there was something to hit, I seemed unerringly to go for it. Then there was the sleeping thing. Now I wasn't only dropping off at night, but at rather embarrassing times of the day, too – like *The*

Independent on Sunday editorial conference. And I felt drunk. Not nice drunk, but head-spin drunk.

Back to Giles. He decided to send me to Ipswich for an MRI scan. These are no fun. First you have to put on a mask, like an ice-hockey goalie. Then you lie still for 40 minutes while what sounds like that ice hockey match goes on around you. "Bang, plunk, plunk." "Just one more," says the radiologist. "Plunk, bang, bang." "That's it, now make an appointment with your neurologist for next week to hear the results."

"Can't you tell me?"

"No, I don't understand these things, I just work the machine."

As if. Still, I suppose that's what they have to say for fear of putting a foot in it.

Back to Giles again the next week. He hasn't called, so it must be clear — mustn't it?

No.

"You've got something. As I'd thought. Look at these blobs on your MRI."

"What are they?"

"We call them blobs."

"There seem to be a lot of them."

"Yes. Not good news, I'm afraid."

"So what is it?"

"I'm not going to tell you right now. I want you to tell me."

And so it began. An hour of cat and mouse. Not cancer, not CJD. By the end, of course, I guessed — if only by elimination. Doubtless Giles was right to make me say the words first. Perhaps that lessens the shock. Anyway, by this time, like me you'll probably have sussed what I've got. It begins with M and ends with S.

Charlie Courtauld will be writing a regular column.

141

The thing about a disease with a name is that you can look it up

7 January 2001

A name is, they say, just a name. I had some symptoms before the medical diagnosis gave a name to them, I have some now. Nothing – on the face of it – is any different.

But of course, it doesn't feel like that. A name on a diagnosis changes everything. For a start, it validates the symptoms – and not only those I've got, but those I have had in the past. Like the time I lost my sense of taste for a month. Or the "RSI" I had in my arm.

Suddenly it all seems to make sense. So – in a way – I welcome the diagnosis. My wife, Lucy, on the other hand, hates it. Right from the start, this thing has come between us: I've got it, she hasn't – and there's nothing that either of us can do about that.

Perhaps the biggest change now that it has been given a name is that I can look it up. Like this:

Multiple sclerosis noun Pathol. a chronic degenerative, often episodic disease of the central nervous system marked by patchy destruction of the myelin that surrounds and insulates nerve fibres, usually appearing in young adulthood and manifested by one or more mild to severe neural and muscular impairments, as spastic weakness in one or more limbs, local sensory losses, bladder dysfunction, or visual disturbances.

The weeks following the diagnosis have been filled with definitions like this. My voracious appetite for information on the disease has been sated by books, dictionaries and – courtesy of an ISDN line and (most importantly) an obliging-despite-being-heavily-pregnant Lucy – the internet. At the click of a mouse, I've learnt everything I wanted to – and rather more.

On the day of the diagnosis I took my first trip to the library. Closed. Next, the bookshop.

"Have you got a health section?"

"Over there."

The health section was huge, groaning with fat hardbacks. I was impressed – until I started perusing them. In the old days, the definition of "health" was fairly straightforward. It was about being unwell. Then the Californians got in on the act. Now, don't get me wrong. I've got nothing against books with titles like "All Men Are Bastards And All Women Are Fantastic" or "HRT – a Gift from Heaven" and so on. But they do rather seem to have taken over the shelves, to the exclusion of the real health books.

In fact, once I'd ploughed past these, and made it through the zillions of books on birth and baby care (most of which we've got at home already) there was only one relevant tome. The title, "Surviving MS", was depressing enough. The decision to use black as the cover's colour was – I felt – off-putting. But the relentlessly upbeat tone, coupled with amusing cartoons about wheelchairs and incontinence took the biscuit. I bought the book anyway. It was all I could get. Lucy and I spent the next few days surreptitiously reading a few pages and then hiding the book from each other.

But after a couple of days Lucy had put out a plea and other, less gruesome books arrived. The black book went in the bin.

These new books were better, but confusing. Some said I should immediately pack in the fags. Another – the one I preferred – said I shouldn't. Some said I must eat only nuts and take masses of vitamins. My preferred tome said "crackpot rubbish". In fact, the more I read of this book, the more I liked it. Until, that is, the last page.

It wasn't the author's fault. He wrote the book in 1987. It must have seemed like a good idea at the time to print a list of role models for MS patients to look up to, aspire towards. But one name brought me to earth with a bump. It hadn't even occurred to me, and ever since I read it, I can't seem to get away from Jacqueline du Pré.

First there was the Christmas shopping to do, and where better to get something for Lucy's stocking than the record shop? But they had a classical promotion on, and, wouldn't you know it, it was Elgar that they were prominently displaying. Not just any Elgar, mind, but the Cello Concerto played by THAT WOMAN. I rushed home, empty-handed and fed up. But at least there was the Christmas viewing to plan. What films are on offer? Not Titanic again! Let's look at Channel 4's blockbuster offering:

9.00 Hilary and Jackie.

Now, ever since our time at Bristol University, I've tried to keep up with Emily Watson's glittering career. She's the great success story of our year. So I was torn. Rubbish on every other side, Emily on 4 – but playing THAT WOMAN.

The television stayed switched off on Christmas night. But names have still dominated the Christmas period. Baby names. This is our third, and it doesn't get any easier. With our two favourite girl's names gone (Daisy and Martha), it is in fact harder. My ritual choices for boy's names are, as usual, vetoed by Lucy (although I still can't fathom her objections to Merlin or Pirate).

With this one, for the first time, we're falling back on one of those baby name books, which I stumbled across while looking for stuff about MS. But the book just makes it harder. How can 6,000 names all be ghastly? But believe me, they are.

"Aaron?"
"No."

"Abigail?"
"No."

"Jacqueline?"
"No way!"

143

Now everyone knows, apart from those who matter most

4 February 2001

Perhaps the most difficult decision of the past few weeks – even greater than choosing a name for the baby (Rory, by the way) – has been deciding whom to tell about my diagnosis, and how.

Early conversations were clumsy. It's not an easy thing to slip into a chat. So the first attempts were hamfisted:

"Charlie. Long time no see. How are you?"

"Fine. Except I've got MS."

"Oh my god!"

End of chatty conversation.

More subtle methods were called for. They were no good, either:

"Charlie. Happy New Year. How goes?"

"Fine. The baby's due any day now. Lucy's looking huge. And, oh yes, I've got Multiple Sclerosis."

"What?"

"Yes, anyway, how are you?"

"Oh my god!"

End of chatty conversation.

You see, it's a problem. Either I blurt it out (conversational death) or I try to be casual and it just comes out weird.

There is an alternative. Not to blab about it. Keep it a secret. But the trouble with that is that it's all I can think about at the moment – so my concentration wanders easily, and I end up not listening to what is being said:

"Hi Charlie. Everything OK?" [Thinks: What does that mean? Does she know?]

"Fine thanks. A good New Year?" [Should I tell her? Is she only being nice because she knows? Does she look like an Independent on Sunday reader? Is that a sympathetic smile, or a smirk? Will I be a cripple soon? Can I get one of those orange parking dispensations? When's the election going to be? When will the builders be out? Is Lucy going to have the baby today? Who is this person?]

"I'm sorry. What?"

All of these techniques have the same basic flaw. They all force everyone into making a BIG DEAL out of this. Inevitably, with the diagnosis so recent, that can't be wholly avoided, but I was keen to find a way of keeping me and Lucy away from other people's reactions. So, we came up with another option: tell everyone – but not personally. Partly it was done via this column: that dealt with over 200,000 people at a stroke. But, alarmingly, not everyone appears to read these pages: believe it or not, readers, there are still one or two weirdos out there who don't subscribe to The Independent on Sunday. Even for those who do, I can't be sure that they've read what I've written about MS.

"Charlie. Loved your piece in the Sindie." [Which one? The one about the SNP – or the one about MS? How can I tell? If you loved that one, you must be a mean bastard. But if you loved the other one, you must be a bit of a political nerd.]

So the second part of the cunning plan was to encourage people to tell each other. Like a chain letter, the news would spread – and I would no longer have to worry about which people know and which don't know. Brilliant. Now we can all get back to our lives.

But now a new problem arises. Almost everyone knows – except some of those who matter the most: my children.

Daisy is four. Martha is two. As I write, Rory is eight hours old, following a fairly gruesome – but ultimately worthwhile – four-hour labour endured by Lucy. (In fact, this was one of the rare occasions when having MS proved an asset. After a tip-off from Lucy, the midwife was almost nice to the husband – something of a first on a labour ward.)

All three children are – I hope – now asleep: the girls upstairs and Rory having his first night in Colchester General. For the moment, Lucy and I are their role models. We are impregnable superheroes, able to move mountains (or at least to demonstrate how to get Pingu to leap across treacherous ice floes in the new CD Rom.)

So, when should we smash that youthful hero-worship by revealing that Daddy is a mere mortal, prone at any time to falling over – even without added alcohol? The question is more pertinent than it sounds. The other day, I allowed Daisy to ride on the back of my bike as I cycled up the lane to pick up the papers. In the process, my vision went haywire and I nearly crashed the bike several times. But to refuse Daisy that fairly innocent pleasure would force me to make a decision without giving Daisy a good reason – something which all dutiful readers of parenting guides are ordered to avoid. Of course, this sort of situation can be fudged: next time I won't tell Daisy that I'm off to get the papers at all. But at some point the announcement will have to be made. Do I do it at a time of my choosing – or when it becomes unavoidable? And do I break it to them all at once, despite the four-and-a-half-year age gap, or do I stagger it – forcing Daisy to keep a secret from her younger siblings?

For the moment, these decisions are in the future. Let's hope they stay that way – long enough at least for Rory to master the mysteries of leg-spin bowling.

When it comes to taste, Pot Noodle dregs is flavour of the day

4 March 2001

"And I've got one, two, three, four, five, senses working overtime ..." warbles Andy Partridge of XTC on most of the singles compilation tapes I made in the early 1980s (usually filling that tricky end-of-side-one slot). This week I've got only one, two, three, four. The non-effect of what should have been a deliciously spiced-up curry on Saturday night marked the disappearance of my taste buds. It wasn't a complete surprise. I lost my taste for a month over the millennium – which saved me from having to knock back glasses of cheap champagne in the Dome. Giles, the neurologist who knows everything there is to know about MS, tells me that losing taste is a "very rare" first symptom – which makes me feel tremendously important, but isn't much help to me at suppertime as I push another plateful away.

My friends are envious. To them, no taste equals no calories equals fitting again into slim clothes from the back of the cupboard. They have a point. I'm certainly not joining them as they panic-buy pork scratchings during this foot and mouth outbreak, and the scales no longer hold the terror that they once did. And I'm blowing the dust off those old lightweight army trousers that were quite trendy back in 1979 and which, courtesy of All Saints, and renamed "cargo pants", are sort of back in vogue again. So if you see a sad Eighties throwback shuffling through the streets these days, that's me (unless it's Limahl from Kajagoogoo).

I often think that taste is an over-rated sense. To put taste and smell on a level with sight, hearing and feeling has always struck me as unfair. But the downside of this symptom is that not everything tastes of water, as everyone assumes. On the contrary, it is that everything, water in particular, tastes of the dregs of a Pot Noodle.

I've always been something of a fussy eater: aubergines, chocolate, anchovies and ham all have a place on my "no thank you" list. But the flipside of that is that if I like a food, I love it. Once a foodstuff – curry, Quavers, a cheese, Marmite and mayo sandwich – has got my tastebuds twitching, I can't get enough of it. Or I couldn't, at any rate. Now even these tempting titbits hold no promise.

At the BBC tea bar, normally a mainstay of my lunch hour, some adman has decided to brand all the sandwiches with an identical, lurid green sticker bearing the single word TASTE. Following the lead of Pret a Manger, the corporation's sandwich makers have come up with ever-more exotic fillings for their slices of bread. They are wasting their time on me: duck pate with basil and mozzarella has an identical TASTE to cardboard with extra wallpaper paste to my refined palate these days. The only thing with much of a residual taste for me is a cigarette – and that's probably only because my Silk Cut ultra milds had no flavour in the first place.

But the good thing about this symptom is that, because I've had it before (and it went away after four weeks), I'm optimistic that its return means I'm due to go into remission. In the majority of cases, multiple sclerosis is a relapsing – remitting disease: it comes and goes. But we've been waiting rather longer than I'd hoped for a remission[1] – hopefully, the loss of taste, which was brief last time, is the beginning of the end of this attack.

Life seems very much a waiting game at the moment. At the BBC, we're waiting for Tony Blair to call an election, primed to deploy our outside broadcast resources and our Peter Snow graphics to bring you the results on the night. At home, Lucy and I are waiting for a month-old Rory to sleep through the night, for two-year-old Martha to discover the joys of her potty and four-year-old Daisy to learn her letters. And, like everyone living out here in the sticks, we're waiting to see how the foot and mouth outbreak develops.[2]

Finally, we're also waiting for next Friday's episode of The Middle Classes on BBC2 to see how the editors have stitched together their interviews with my father and me. I've been in the business long enough to know that juxtaposing tension makes good TV – and that means disagreement. Now, I can accept that my father and I don't see eye-to-eye on absolutely everything – but can they have made us look like a pair of buffoons? The signs weren't good when the producer sent me off to put on a suit and tie for the interview. And the producer's letter this week, telling us that the best bits are on the cutting-room floor, has really set alarm bells ringing: so they only used the worst bits? How will this programme affect our family – a pertinent question at the best of times, and yet more relevant given that we live only a few hundred yards apart.

There's an added twist to this anticipation: the interview was carried out after this MS attack had begun, but before the diagnosis was made. How will the post-diagnosis me react to the happy-go-lucky, ignorant me on the screen?

Meanwhile, in the words of XTC, I carry on "trying to taste the difference between lemon and lime". Between lemon and milk would be a start.

[1] Charlie never actually went into remission, and was later diagnosed with progressive MS.
[2] See blog entry 72.

While we wait, the experts can't even decide when to decide

1 April 2001

Less than keen on any lottery that would not pay for its big tent by the Thames, New Labour came to office promising to end the "postcode lottery" in the NHS. This was the system whereby local health authorities could choose their own priorities for drug prescriptions – and it has led to wide disparities across the country.

So Tony Blair set up the National Institute for Clinical Excellence. Nice for short: a nice name for nice people. Or so we are supposed to think. But Nice has turned nasty to those of us with multiple sclerosis; we await a decision as to whether or not the drugs that may lessen the frequency of our attacks are value for money – and so can be prescribed. So far, Nice has deliberated for more than two years, and come to no conclusion. Its latest estimate for an announcement is sometime around November.

In a former guise, I was editor of the BBC's Question Time. During my tenure, the edition that generated the most headlines was broadcast on 8 July 1998. That was when the Prime Minister, caught off-guard by a question on fox hunting, made the pledge to ban the sport, a decision he must now regret. I mention this only because there was another question addressed to him that night which has become significant for me. Unlike Mr Blair's remarks on hunting, this issue, however, has been widely ignored. During a discussion about NHS waiting lists, a grey-haired woman in the audience put her hand up to speak to the Prime Minister.

"May I suggest one way of reducing your waiting lists to go into hospital is to make sure that multiple sclerosis patients have the benefit of beta interferon? It has been proven they won't have to go into hospital so often," she said.

TB: "Well thank you for your suggestion. I'm not qualified actually to answer on it. But if I can make the more general point, there are all sorts of things you can do to reduce waiting lists."

Woman: "May I suggest that that answer does not address the question. Patients should not have to be at that level (waiting). They should be helped before they need hospitalisation."

"If you leave me your name I will write to you."

"I have written to you. It took eight weeks to get a reply."

Oh dear. I knew this question would arise, even if it took Mr Blair by surprise. Every Question Time audience member can suggest two questions. The fact that this redoubtable person had taken the unusual step of suggesting identical questions on beta interferon left no doubt that the subject would arise if the opportunity came; a discussion on waiting lists was just what she needed.

What I didn't know then, of course, was that I'd soon find myself on that beta interferon waiting list – and I am somewhere near the bottom of Essex Rivers Health Authority's list.

Since that day, along with every other MP, Mr Blair has had to educate himself about MS drugs; and they have become something of a political hot potato. Even William Hague has noticed, and was prompted to ask a Commons question about them. But from Nice, no decision. It can't even decide when it will decide, as the putative date for an announcement is delayed yet again. All of which means that I, along with thousands of others, have faced the unpalatable choice of either waiting on or paying for the drugs. Giles, the neurologist, thinks that Nice will decide against prescribing – so I'm taking the latter course.

Just as the market takes a nosedive, my mother is flogging her remaining stocks to fund my £500-a-month supply of a drug called Copaxone. It's half the price of interferon. But even coughing up loads of dosh for a daily jab isn't as easy as it sounds. Before I can get my uncontrollably shaking hands (is it excitement or tremor?) on the phials of this precious stuff, I have to undergo more tests to check my suitability. Blood is drawn. My white cell count is high. Isn't that good? Chest X-rays are snapped. Er, why?

A wait for the results. Then even after the magical prescription is written out by Giles, I need to make a booking to be taught how to inject myself with the valuable fluid every morning without pumping it straight into a vein by mistake. Space for the tubes must be found in the fridge out of the reach of prying daughters – so it's farewell to that manky lump of past-its-date mozzarella.

Of course, the sting in the Nice tale is that the committee's rulings do not cover Scotland or Northern Ireland, anyway. As it has done with student fees and long-term nursing care, and is now on the point of doing with measles jabs, the Scottish parliament will undoubtedly cock a snook at Westminster by allowing beta interferon prescriptions north of the border. This go-ahead is especially likely since (for reasons that remain unclear) Scotland is MS-land: it has twice the proportion of cases that we have in England.

So it may be time to flip through those Country Life Scottish house adverts, and dream of moving to Lochinver. Long live the postcode McLottery!

Pecs, rowing machines and sweat: no gym'll ever fix it for me
29 April 2001

I'm sure that you, like me, keep mental lists of things that you intend never to do in your lifetime Unbreakable Life Maxims. They are a mixture of sensible tips ULM 1: "I will never play Russian roulette" and personal prejudices ULM 7: "I will never play anything by Santana". Always fairly high on my list has been an aversion to exercise, and particularly to gyms ULM 3: "I will never, ever, set foot in a gym". Except for a few embarrassments with bars and ropes at school, it was a rule I'd managed to adhere to. Until now.

Perhaps the defining moment in this aversion was exposure, while in my formative teenage years, to university flat-mates caught up in the risible fashion for leg-warmers, possessing copies of Jane Fonda workout tapes and addicted to awful movies such as Dirty Dancing and, most horribly, Perfect, in which Jamie Lee Curtis discovers the joys of the rowing machine. I was scarred for life. For me, then, one of the most unpleasant conclusions of my multiple sclerosis diagnosis came not from the neurologist, but from the physiotherapist. "It's important to build up the muscle in your arms and legs. Lots of exercise. Are you a member of a gym?"

The Essex Health Club is situated on a Second World War airfield. One's first impressions are that the Germans did a pretty accurate job of targeting the site, leaving hideous craters everywhere. Sadly, no: that's the golf course. And that architectural bad dream in the middle of the car park must be the gym.

The car park is heaving, but with my new disabled parking badge, I can manoeuvre right next to the chalet. This blue badge is enormous, reminiscent of those charity cheques that businessmen hand over on Comic Relief night. But the badge has the desired effect of stopping the bolshie parking attendant in his tracks, before he can send me to a vacant slot three miles away. He slinks away, cursing.

I walk into the club and stumble past piles of golf trousers, balls and even left-hand-only gloves for sale. Into the gym. Bye-bye, Unbreakable Life Maxim 3. First, dispel any notions picked from Jamie Lee Curtis that gyms might be sexy. The acres of sweat and flab on display are anything but. In fact, the be-thonged women look less reminiscent of Jamie Lee after a shower than of her mother, Janet Psycho Leigh, in the shower of the Bates motel after Norman has had his fun with a knife.

To avoid a sudden MS attack, it is necessary not to raise my temperature unduly. As a result, my circuit at the gym is embarrassingly easy: no more than four minutes on any piece of kit. Hence, while the other members of the Essex Club spend hours in skimpy shorts and T-shirts drenched with sweat, I'm able to do my entire routine without taking my jersey off. Not only that, old ladies gasp in horror when, after they've spent 20 minutes pumping 150lbs on the rowing machine, I saunter over and reduce the weight to 70lbs for my two minutes. Nevertheless, after a couple of minutes on the treadmill my temperature has risen enough to ensure that I'm staggering around like a drunkard, my vision and balance gone.

Actually, the effect on my vision is not entirely unwelcome, since the view out of the club window is particularly depressing: one half-filled skip and a putting green covered with hundreds of men mis-hitting balls. Never having played golf myself, it looks all too easy to get the ball in the hole from five feet, which makes it toe-curlingly irritating to watch people fail time and again. If something is that hard, it can't be worth doing, let alone paying for.

Turning my attention away from the window, I am faced by a bank of telly screens. Now, being something of a television addict, you might think I'd welcome the opportunity of some quality time with the box. And, indeed, I did time my weekly excursions to the club to coincide with David Frost's Sunday chats on the sofa. However, the club's management seems to have decided that although you may watch TV while pumping iron, you may not hear it. So I am left with the sight of Frostie and guests goldfishing about the events of the week. But all I can hear is ... what is that din?

Back in the 1970s, Brian Eno released a series of muzak albums Music For Airports, Music For Lifts, Music For Films etc. But he omitted Music For Health Clubs. That vacuum has now been filled, alas, ("Cause I am your laydeeeee") by compilation tapes of 1980s power anthems ("Who's gonna drive you hoooooome tonight?") played at top volume ("Take my breath awaaaaay"). Nigel from Spinal Tap would surely approve of these speakers, which seem stuck on 11 ("Everything I do, I do it foooooooor you"). At least, I suppose that they have the desired effect since the crashing guitar sounds ensure that everyone cracks on with their pec-enhancement regime and gets out of the gym as soon as possible. But not before checking to see if they have moved up the ladders which adorn the walls, one marking VO2 scores whatever they are and the other showing the frequency of attendance. Unlikely ever to feature in either of these competitions, I am free to marvel at the dedication/insanity? of those vying for the top spot, who hit the treadmill about 28 times a month.

My routine complete, it's time to go. Time, too, to come up with a new Unbreakable Life Maxim 3. How about "I will never buy Ian Lang's autobiography". Pretty safe, you might think. Until you discover that I've got two copies of Norman Fowler's.

151

At last I've found an excuse for my famous cack-handedness

27 May 2001

I am a lefty and, for those of you fed up with reading about the election, that has nothing to do with my political views. No, it refers to my leftish leanings with a pen. The near-illegible scrawl that comes from my left hand may persuade you otherwise, but that's before you've seen the efforts from my right. Already my four-year-old daughter, Daisy, can write better with her right than I can, and that's after only one lesson. For all the important tasks in life – bowling a cricket ball, drinking a coffee, smoking cigarettes, bottle-feeding a baby or picking my nose – my left hand is the natural choice.

But that didn't stop my primary school headmaster from imposing a ruthless purge of this leftish tendency. Like one of those Bible Belt classroom creationists who throw Darwin's books into the dustbin, my head didn't believe in newfangled theories – such as left-handedness. Through my form teacher, Miss Roy, the edict was sent that all pupils must learn to write properly, and that meant from the right.

Miss Roy was something of a local heroine in north Essex. Long before Channel 4 noticed the fact, she realised that teachers can be cool and sexy. Her short skirts and thigh-high leather boots sent fathers' pulses racing on sports day. She was also the closest we had to a celebrity, since her father was rarely off Look East, being interviewed about his unfeasibly long moustache. The curled whiskers earned him a place in the Guinness Book of Records (a British record only, alas – he never came close to the Chinese world champion) and he even once showed his tufts on Blue Peter.

But, however famous she might have been, Miss Roy's classes were a horror to endure. Forced to hold my Platignum italic pen in an uncomfortable way, and chant the mantra "right is right, left is wrong", I found shaping my letters an impossibility. My handwriting looked worse and worse until the only career paths that seemed open to me were in teaching journalists to scrawl shorthand or GPs to write prescriptions.

Eventually my parents were forced to march me off to a shrink. I don't know his name, but I do remember that, like all self-respecting psychiatrists in the 1970s, he had a thick Polish accent. He did the standard inkblot tests (quite why, I'll never know), and duly wrote a letter to the effect that I was hugely left-hand dominant and that forcing me to write with my right was detrimental to my mental wellbeing. Surely this evidence would convince my headmaster – and so he was shown the shrink's note.

"Nonsense," was the considered response. I didn't stay at the school much longer. Ever since, I have ploughed the traditional clumsy furrow of the cack-handed. I am unable to handle china without dropping it, or drive a car without crashing. Hitherto, supported by a book titled The Left Hander Syndrome, I have blamed the conspiracy of the right-handed for these breakages. If only the world were more lefty-friendly, I have moaned, these disasters wouldn't happen. (This confidence was rather shattered when, on a visit to the Left-Handed Shop in Soho, I discovered that a lifetime in this

152

right-handed world had left me entirely unable to use the left-handed tin openers and cheque books on display.)

But now I have a new excuse. A dropped plate, a dented car door, a smashed mirror – it's all because I've got multiple sclerosis. Never mind that I've always been a clumsy git: henceforward all breakages are down to this disease.

And, 30 years on from that primary school, I have at last a reason to thank Miss Roy for her stubbornness. Most of the symptoms of my MS have subsided for now, just in time for the election (which is a massive relief, because I'm working like a dog at the moment). But I have still got a very annoying tremor in my left arm. This isn't like the shakes you might get from over-indulging in caffeine: my arm constantly jerks in an alarming fashion, so much so that there's apparently a rumour at the BBC's Westminster offices, where I'm working, that I've got an out-of-control cocaine habit.

But the tremor means that, for many tasks, my trusty left arm is now a no-no and so – for the first time since Miss Roy's form – I'm using my right instead.

Last week, fed up with the sight of undecorated plasterwork on the outside of the garage, I finally bought a brush from Travis Perkins, changed into the overalls that my wife, Lucy, gave me for Christmas (hint, hint) and did some painting with my right hand.

OK, so most of the paint fell on the ground or daubed my hair, but at last I succeeded in getting the garage walls white. Lucy and I had hoped that this would give alfresco summer lunches a Mediterranean flavour. Unfortunately, until we get some plants growing up them, the relentless white walls are more evocative of a 19th century loony bin (or, even worse, BBC Television Centre). But at least I did it. Miss Roy would be proud. Right is, after all, right.

Patient, stab thyself

24 June 2001

After weeks of to-ing and fro-ing between my GP, my neurologist, X-ray departments and blood testers, I finally got the prescription from my multiple sclerosis guru, Giles. It was Giles who'd first recommended the stuff, Copaxone, but the delicacies of the NHS meant that my GP, Dennis, was lumbered with the task of collecting the data – even though the NHS won't pay for MS drugs so, via Giles again, I have to pay £130 a week to get it privately.

With the prescription signed, I assumed that I'd soon be on the medication. Not so fast. First I had to book in for a delivery. As with all deliveries these days their proposed time was breathtakingly inconvenient – 10am, just as I was due to arrive at work, and while Lucy was between taking one daughter to school and the other to nursery – via baby Rory's weekly weighing session.

Fortunately, my parents were at home, only a couple of doors away, so I got the package detoured to their house instead. And what a consignment. Naively, perhaps, I had assumed that a delivery of medicine was rather like a delivery of pornography – small, discreetly wrapped, unassuming. Not a bit of it: this was more like an Ikea kitchen – loads of brightly-coloured parts and no instruction manual. Here's what I unpacked: 1 yellow bin for disposal of sharp bits, to be kept away from children (How, when Daisy is convinced it contains Smarties?) 1 blue pack of Copaxone, to keep safe in the fridge. (How, when Martha says it looks like a box of choccies?) 28 phials of distilled water, 28 syringes, 40 enormous needles, 40 not-so-big-but-still-pretty-huge needles, 1 instruction video, 1 ice pack and carry bag (like you take sandwiches to the seaside in) So, everything unpacked, on with the video. Now, those of us who work in television have long been sneery about corporate videos, so it was with expectations of wobbly camerawork and antediluvian editing that I pressed play. It was even worse. I had thought "zany" graphic devices such as "page turns" or "clock wipes" had gone to the great test card in the sky, but no, here they were again as insanely happy MS patients – surrounded by cheerful children – learned to mix and inject with Copaxone.

But while the presentation was soothingly ham-fisted, the actors were anything but. They were brilliant, extracting fluid from upside-down bottles, sticking needles into their perma-tanned bodies with one hand in a quick, painless motion (thus leaving the other hand free to change nappies, cook dinner or knock off a novel). How could I hope to emulate their perfect technique?

Anyway, I've got the stuff, I've endured the video: can I start? Nope – I had to be trained first. With a carful of tired children and a pissed-off husband in tow, a nurse turns up to ensure that I can do it properly. Slowly, carefully, she took me through the procedure. It's fairly simple really, although by the time she'd finished, my checklist of things to do – all in the right order – stretched to 24 items. Doubtless the knowledge I have to pay a fortune for a daily stab in the arm kept my attention from wandering. But finally, I'd got it. The girls were in bed, the chickens roosting, the house quiet. Time for my first solo jab. Just as I was steeling myself, the phone rang.

"Hi, Giles here."

"Oh Giles. Glad you called. You're just in time for the first injection."

"Er…"

"OK, so I've got the phone in one hand, and this bloody great needle in the other. This was your idea, so you can keep me company while I jab myself."

"Um… Er…"

"OK. Here we go. I've got my shirt off. Rub the sweat away, take aim and – into the tummy it goes. Ow ow ow ow. This is all your fault. Push the syringe down. In goes the Copaxone – brrr, rather cold – and… out it comes. My god that hurt, you bastard. Now: what can I do for you?"

"Er… Perhaps I've got the wrong number… Is Geoff there?"

"Oh, sorry. I thought you were another Giles. Geoff moved out a year ago."

Click. Brrrr.

Me and my celebrity pals

22 July 2001

"When will I, will I be famous?" So asked those bottle-blond boys from Bros back in 1988. To nobody's surprise (except perhaps theirs), the answer was that their 60 seconds of fame were already ticking away, trumping Andy Warhol's prediction. The brothers from Fife haven't been heard of since, except for brief reprises on BBC2's "I love the 80s" nights.

The reason I mention the fickle finger of fame is that, in my bored, nothing-to-do-so-I'll-type-my-name-into-an-internet-search-engine moments, I have recently found myself in a list entitled "Famous People with Multiple Sclerosis". At first, this struck me as rather flattering. Alongside me in the "C" section is Michael Crichton, The creator of ER and *Jurassic Park*. But who else are my celebrity chums in illness? Carrel Cowan-Ricks, an archaeologist, Betty Cuthbert, sprinter, Luca Coscoine, Italian politician, and Sean Coman, Californian disc jockey. Notable about this list is that – with the exception of Mr Crichton – nobody has ever heard of any of us. We're each household names – but only in our own households.

All of this suggests that the website authors were rather scratching around for some celebrity glamour to attach to our medical condition: a message rather contrary to the one they hoped to convey. The idea of publishing a list of celebs with MS has two flaws: first, the most famous MS sufferer – Jacqueline du Pré – is dead, and therefore hardly an inspiration to the rest of us. Second (again with the exception of Mr Crichton), too few living MS patients are famous. Ah, how we wish for a truly superstar victim. A Kate Winslet, a Spice Girl, a Tim Henman…. A hint of razzle-dazzle like that, the argument goes, might jolt the government which, because of the cost, still insists on denying us the medicines we need. And so we wait, grimly hoping that a chart-popping starlet or best-selling author soon gets the bad news.

This is the second occasion on which I've attracted a dubious kind of celebrity status. A couple of years ago, during my tenure as editor of the BBC's *Question Time*, I was phoned at home by a hack from an obscure magazine called *Heat*. They had noticed that the *Question Time* panels sometimes included a sprinkle of stardust: the usual crop of Anne Widdicombes, Alistair Darlings and Roy Jenkingses were sometimes supplemented by a Nigella Lawson or a Billy Bragg. To my mind this was a natural extension of the *Question Time* format: interesting people debating the issues of the day in an interesting way.

The Heat journalist wanted to know how far I would go in following my own logic. Trying to make the idea understandable for Heat's core readership of Baby Spice wannabes, I suggested that providing that she had interesting things to say, even an expatriate starlet would be welcome if she brought her own safety pins.

Well, the article duly appeared, and I was quite pleased with it. OK, so they had rather ramped up my ambitions in the headline "Liz Hurley set to appear on *Question Time*", but the quotes were accurate, and *Heat*'s few readers might be amused enough to give the old programme another try.

However, the story was then picked up. Within a few days, I was named by the broadsheets as the architect of the BBC masterplan to dumb down our once great BairdVision. Various wiseacres such as Gerald Kaufman predicted an end to sentient life as we know it. Other dunderheads vowed never to appear on the programme again. Actually, this news was not at all unwelcome: the "never again" crowd were led by arch-dullard Ruth Lea, an economist of such profound dreariness that I would willingly have walked over broken glass not to invite her back.

Nevertheless, the media attention did give me a taste of the life which our A-list colleagues must live: any misunderstood nuance or literally-taken joke will find its way into a po-faced leading article. It's not a glamourous way to live. So, a star I am not. Not even a wannabe. Don't expect to see me opening your village fête next year, or inviting Hello! readers into my sumptuous dining-room. No, look for me in my rightful place – "Unknowns with MS".

Proud to be a hypocrite

19 August 2001

Flick through the pages of any paper and you'll discover that a new crime has been added to the list. Hypocrisy. It's the excuse for a thousand Fleet Street stings. But is it so bad?

I speak as a practised hypocrite. Only last weekend, Lucy and I assembled a troupe of friends at St Margaret's C of E Church, Gosfield, after the morning service had finished. We filed in for the baptism of our baby boy, Rory. Candles were lit, sermons made, promises delivered. All very harmless, all very English. A wall of gravestones marks the plots where generations of my family rest in peace. The only flaw? I don't believe in God. To me, the service was a catalogue of gobbledygook. It would be great to believe that there is a heaven, a happy retirement home for nice people and house-trained pug dogs. But I'm afraid that the idea stretches my credulity to breaking point.

It was not ever thus. There was a time – when I was around 16 – when I suffered what can only be described as a crisis of atheism. For a while, I started going to extra church services, offering to make the readings, ring the bells, mix the wine. Not only that, I opted to take an A-level in Divinity, hoping that by careful Bible study I would move closer to grace. But the effect was opposite. The A-level course called for close textual analysis of four Bible books: two from the Old Testament, two from the New.

The OT books first, Amos and Hosea. Two of the biggest bores ever to walk the Holy Land in bare feet. To his credit, Hosea came up with that line about sowing the wind and reaping the whirlwind, but otherwise this miserable duo wrote the most dreary catalogues of doom imaginable. How the editors of the Bible allowed these books to slip through I'll never know.

From the New Testament, it was Luke and Acts. The miraculous meanderings of Saul and Jesus left me unmoved. I stopped going to church: someone else was brought in to mix the drinks and pull the ropes. But I stuck with the A-level course: after all, it was supposedly dead easy to get a top grade.

And so it stood, for years. Lucy and I elected not to get married in church. The Henley register office did the deed. We went to church on family occasions, but did so without feeling too hypocritical. But then that christening question arose. Not, at first, with regard to our own children but with friends' babies. The road to hypocrisy hell began with a phone call from Lucy and James, who had just had their first baby: "Hi, Lucy here. James and I would be very honoured [oh, oh – here it comes] if you'd agree to be one of Dudley's godfathers."

"Me? Lovely. But I don't believe in God."

"No worries. Nor do the others. It doesn't matter at all these days."
"Oh. In that case I'd be delighted." And so a place was reserved for me in hell.

Since then, I've accepted three more such invitations, for Emily, Sophie and Con (who has yet to be christened). Each time, I've trooped into the church, mumbled the obligatory words and gone back for a delicious lunch and prezzie fest. We've followed the same procedure with our kids, now all duly christened. And how lovely it's been: nobody hurt, everyone happy.

But the first faltering steps on the slippery slope to full-blown hypocrisy had been taken. Once your child is christened, and has watched a few episodes of Bear in the Big Blue House (Channel 5 kids' output), it's time to think about schooling. And if, like us, you live out in the sticks, you may discover that the Church of England (as part of its get- 'em-young recruitment policy) has all but monopolised the village school system. At least we don't have to be regular attenders to get Daisy a place. Under those circumstances I don't know what I'd do. Yes, I do. I'd cross my fingers and turn up, like the confirmed hypocrite I am. And in my Divinity A-level? I got a measly C. God can spot a hypocrite. See you in hell, Hamiltons.

I'm still not stoned, alas

11 November 2001

I tried to start a rumour the other day. It was a great rumour. Like all the best, it had an aura of credibility about it. But I haven't heard it since, so I suppose that my career in rumour-mongering is a flop. The idea was that Osama bin Laden had somehow (I hadn't quite worked that bit out) adulterated the world's cocaine supply with anthrax. You can see the perfection – a white powder that City people sniff mixed with a white powder that kills them. And it might – if widely believed – have the beneficial knock-on effect of glassy-eyed cokeheads stopping their habit of handing over their cash to Colombian murderers.

But starting a rumour isn't as easy as you might think. The problem was that although the idea was great, I hadn't a clue how to get the gossip going. I wasn't about to join the internet chat-room crowd of weirdos. And there was the worry that I might be giving ideas to cranks. So a flaw arose in my plan. I didn't tell anyone, which rather destroys the point.

Drugs have been on my mind recently. On my mind, but not in it, unfortunately. I had hoped that I'd be too stoned to write this piece. By now, I'd anticipated that I'd be taking daily doses of cannabis and perhaps couldn't be bothered to get out of bed. But it hasn't worked out like that. My supplier, the National Health Service, hasn't delivered yet. So I'm still stone-cold sober, I'm afraid. Even though I bump into things like a drunkard.

For I had hoped that I'd be a willing statistic in that trial of cannabis for multiple sclerosis sufferers. My neurologist, Giles, was going to put me forward for it but the health authority has stymied that route by the brilliant manoeuvre of suspending Giles from the NHS. He had the temerity to question its wisdom in allocating only one consultant neurologist for our region, which meant that his waiting list was 14 months long. The upshot? Giles got suspended for his rudeness, and there is now no NHS consultant for this area. Giles is kicking his heels at home while a couple of hapless locums try to plough through his list. Meanwhile, I have had to apply direct to the cannabis trial people to get on their little list. It's a lot harder than just going out and buying the weed from a bloke in a bedsit.

There is always a price to be paid for going on these trials. Yes, you might get early free and legal access to the potion that can put your walking back on the straight and narrow. But you might not. As with most drug trials, this is a "double blind" job. I might get cannabis – or they might give me placebo. There are probably a few kids out there who think that Placebo is the happening new drug. "Like, I was really P'd up, man."

As like as not, I'll get a handy supply of the favoured substitute – sugar. At least you don't have to inject this stuff: I'd be really cheesed off to discover that I was jabbing sugar. But there's another, more disruptive, price. If I go on this trial, I can't drive a car for three months. And out here in the countryside, that matters. After a head-on meeting back in July, I don't have a car at the moment anyway.

In some ways, I suppose a three-month driving ban would be a relief: I'm a crap driver. But it does seem a bit rich that my enforced passenger-ship comes not as a result of my ignorance of the highway code, but because I'll be taking daily doses of – probably – sugar. And there's a third worry: I haven't even taken anything angst-inducing yet. Maybe I should keep my head down just now. I don't want to do anything that'll annoy Alan Milburn. Last week the Department of Health announced that it's planning a countrywide trial of the MS drugs Beta Interferon and Copaxone. It sounds too good to be true: a trial for 10,000 with nobody on sugar? I'm a perfect candidate for Copaxone. So perfect that I'm already on it, courtesy of my mother's bank manager.

So is Santa Alan going to let me have my drugs on the NHS free as part of this so-called "trial"? Or is he just faking it to get himself some good headlines? It's only a rumour.

I am the guru of suffering

9 December 2001

Looking for an answer to the Meaning of Life, Death and the Working Families' Tax Credit? Look no further. For yea, your guru is here. Until about this time last year, I walked in the valley of the ignorant, sounding off about issues of politics and current affairs through a glass, darkly. But now? Now, courtesy of my diagnosis, the scales have fallen from my eyes. For yes, I have joined the ranks of The Suffering, and surely my thoughts are now endowed with a new wisdom and insight. Ever since Job had all those Biblical boils and frogs to put up with, the notion of the nobility of suffering has been deeply ingrained into our psyche. But here's my shameful secret: suffering isn't noble. It doesn't make you wise. This column is just the same old claptrap.

Hurrying home to catch *Newsnight* one evening a while ago, I was beaten up in Askew Road, west London. The perpetrators were caught – and then released by a magistrate, whereupon they skipped the country. Now, given the choice, I'd have chosen to have that magistrate dropped from a great height, and the muggers' fingernails extracted. Fortunately, I wasn't given the choice. Anybody who remembers the electrifyingly vengeful testimony of the Eappen family during the trial of Louise Woodward must be aware that suffering can skew your rationality. Victims of violent crime are the last people to offer a Solomonesque judgement on their case.

And the same applies to medical suffering. For those of us with MS, the prospects for cloned stem cell research are awesome, offering the chance, perhaps, one day, of a cure. Embryonic cells, injected into our brains, could be persuaded to regenerate our battered heads. Which makes it impossible for us to offer a dispassionate view: I'd be all for the compulsory harvesting of stem cells from your children, if I thought that this might find a cure.

At first glance, there is always a temptation for legislators to bow to the views of patients when decision-making. After all, patients are usually well-informed about their condition, and up-to-date about research. To defer to their knowledge could seem both cheap and democratic. But it isn't. Too much knowledge is an expensive thing. So the Government has set up complicated pseudo-democratic "consultation" procedures which – they hope – will give it credit for "listening", while deflecting the blame on to quangos when accused of ignoring victims' pleas.

My friend Anne serves on the board of a mental health trust, and, as part of their remit, they must hold regular open meetings. All very "democratic". Only it isn't. Unsurprisingly, the only people who turn up to a mental health trust's meetings are monomaniacs from the green ink brigade. They may know a lot – but there's a good reason why they aren't on the board.

The same applies to those of us with MS. Ministers have handed the decision over to the "open" decision-making of their Nice committee, with full consultation and appeals procedures. The committee have spent the past three years deliberating, consulting, hearing appeals – and coming to the decision which ministers wanted: that Interferon and Copaxone are too expensive for the NHS to provide.

My problem with all this is not that the wrong decision is arrived at: I'm parti pris on that score anyway. It is that this appearance of "democracy" is nothing of the kind. The consultation is not genuine – and neither are the consultees.

All of which may offer a pointer to the shape of Mr Blair's plans for a future "democratic" House of Lords. Most of the criticism hitherto has assumed that the Prime Minister will pack the chamber with cronies. I think that's unlikely – Downing Street is far too canny. A more likely scenario is that the Lords will be crammed with vociferous – and mutually exclusive – "special interest groups". Imagine the mock-disappointed faces on the Government benches in the Commons when the MPs are "forced" to make a decision over the heads of the quibbling lordships: a decision which ministers had long since decided on anyway.

So don't look to me for wise and impartial decisions. There is nothing wisdom-conferring about pain. It's just painful.

Rory ate my pot plant plant

13 January 2002

"Is it in your family?" It's the first question most people ask about multiple sclerosis, and it's one of the hardest to answer. Some people, brought up on the cod genetics they've picked up from children's TV, have a view that MS is like haemophilia was to Queen Victoria's kids: a familial scourge that gets passed from generation to generation. But it's not like that at all. My parents haven't got it. Nor my grandparents. Nor my siblings. The official word on multiple sclerosis is that genetics does play a part in its transmission, but no one is sure what.

The disease apparently pops up from time to time unexpectedly, and then goes away again. I have a feeling that my grandfather's second cousin August* had it but I'm not sure. Next Saturday will be my chance to find out.

From time to time, readers have been kind/bored enough to write to me, telling me that my experience of the condition is by no means atypical. Indeed, their symptoms are usually more extreme than mine, in a "been-there-done-that-got-the-T-shirt" sort of way. If I lose my sense of taste, a writer tells me they've lost their smell, too. If I fall into an oncoming bike, they've tipped on to a railway line. And so on. So it is with some trepidation that I claim that next Saturday I will do something none of you can match. I'm going to the funeral of my great-great-great-great-great-grandmother. Beat that.

The truth is more prosaic than the boast. A decade ago, Christ Church in Spitalfields decided to clear out the crypt to create a drop-in centre for drop-outs. Among the bodies was that of Louisa Perina Courtauld, Huguenot silversmith (1729-1807). After a few years tinkering with the ossified remains, the British Museum handed them over to cousin Christopher for reburial. And so all of Louisa Perina's descendants have been invited to assemble at Gosfield church for a funeral and burial service on Saturday.

Which begs a question. What's the protocol for the funeral of a long-dead relative? I'm planning to take my kids along: it'll be something for them to tell their grandkids about. But they've not been to a funeral before. Too sad, too mournful. But is this one going to be sad? After 200 years? Surely nobody there will even remember anyone who remembered her? On the other hand, they took their religion seriously, those Huguenots. They were prepared to fight, to kill and die, to flee their country for it. The fact that I couldn't give a toffee shouldn't ... oh, I dunno.

For me, one of the most interesting facets of the occasion will be pseudo-scientific. To meet lots of new relations and to ask them if any of their brood has got MS. It would be futile – but still interesting – to know that Great-Great-Uncle Albert had it too. In those days it probably didn't even have a name. "Mysterious nervous disorder", or something.

But it probably won't help my children, or their cousins for that matter, to avoid the disease. That's because genetics isn't the whole answer. A genetic component, yes.

But others, too. I read somewhere that it is now thought that excessive cleanliness in the teenage years has something to do with it. Having spent my formative years in the communal showers and tetanus-and-splinter-laden classrooms of Eton College, I somehow doubt that.

Meanwhile, the search for a miracle cure or at least something to stop me acting quite so drunkenly when I'm perfectly sober goes on. Haven't heard from the cannabis trial for a while, so I bought some seeds from a bloke in Spitalfields market. Twenty quid for a pack which contained only five seeds seemed a bit of a rip-off to me. Still, with visions of myself as a latter-day Rosie Boycott, I planted them. Nothing. Four of them died without even germinating. From one seed, I did get a weedy-looking sprout. I even gave it a name, Trevor. Encouraged by the sun's feeble midwinter rays, Trevor developed a couple of leaves. After a month, he managed the spectacular height of ... 1in. I had to keep the illegal item hidden over Christmas lest it be recognised by a visitor and reported to the Old Bill.

Yesterday morning, however, I dived out of bed and rushed downstairs to tend my ailing friend. The sight that greeted me was tragic. Our 11-month old son, Rory, held my precious plant pot. It was empty. He had mud all over his mouth. Of Trevor, no sign.

Explorer Augustine Courtauld

• Explorer, Augustine Courtauld (1904-1959) was diagnosed with MS in his forties. He was buried at sea just a few years later, from the Lifeboat he gave to Walton and Frinton stations.

165

Neurologists anonymous

17 February 2002

Have you got a spare? Back-of-a-lorry job? A neurologist, I mean. You see, I seem to have lost mine, and I don't quite know what to do about it.

For most of us, to be signed up to an NHS neurologist is something to be avoided. It means you're not quite right in the head. But just now I could do with one. And, courtesy of Essex Rivers Healthcare Trust, they're a bit thin on the ground up here – ever since my multiple sclerosis guru, Giles, got the heave-ho from Colchester General for being rude. Rude? Is that even worse than being a "wrecker"? Haven't they seen bully-boy Meyer in Holby City, or egghead Romano in ER? Brilliant consultants are supposed to have what Human Resources staff call "poor people skills". Kind of like government special advisers. Even Jo Moore knows that. The more offhand they are, the more brilliant they must be. But managers at this health trust haven't been watching enough TV. So they got rid of Giles, and now I'm in a sort of limbo. Neurologistless. In a state of Neurologistlessness.

Which would be fine, really – I rarely go to the neurologist anyway – but Alan Milburn's made it rather important that I get one. The Health Secretary's announcement last week that – despite the dud advice he got from the Government's own Nice committee – he is going ahead with allowing NHS prescription of the MS drugs Beta Interferon and Copaxone (my one) means that I have to get a neurologist who can write one of those precious NHS prescriptions. What Milburn announced is actually rather canny, on the face of it. The NHS will pay for up to 10,000 of us to get the drugs – but only if the medicinal compounds are seen to do their stuff. If they aren't as efficacious as the companies promise, then the health service will withdraw funding – and the companies will bear the cost instead.

The devil is, as always, in the detail. How is Alan going to find his 10,000 suitable recipients without a massive boost in the number of neurologists? How is the long-term efficacy of these injections to be assessed? Wheelchair demand? The desire for successful treatments may bias doctors and drug companies towards the mildest cases. And, most significantly, what of those poor sods – you, perhaps, or your kids – who are yet to be diagnosed with MS? There doesn't seem to be any accounting for them in the proposal. It's a bit like one of those "Hurry, hurry, offer must end Friday" ads that Brucie does on Boxing Day for Courts furniture. Having dizzy spells? Eyesight problems? My advice is: don't delay, get yourself diagnosed with MS quick, before this once-in-a-lifetime bonanza ends.

These drugs aren't a cure. There isn't one yet. And they cost a packet. Hence the Nice committee's reluctance to recommend them. But they do apparently make relapses less frequent and, right now, they're the only straws we've got to clutch at. Hence, via a fantastically arcane route – Israel, Hungary, courier company – I'm paying for the drugs privately. Which surely must suggest that I'm an ideal candidate for them – unless I've been wasting my mother's and mother-in-law's money for the past year.

But it leaves me with a dilemma. Do I follow Giles to his new NHS post in London – which will involve journeys up to the Big Smoke to see him – or do I register with a new bloke (they are all men, of course. Seen Holby City, have you?) in Ipswich, Bury St Edmunds or Addenbrooke's in Cambridge?

As it happens, I'm due to spend a week in Addenbrooke's next month anyway. My daughter, aged three, has congenital displacement of the hips. That means, according to the admirably rude paediatric consultant, that she may develop wonky walking or get arthritis by the age of 20. Her hip joints were straight "like a toffee apple" rather than bent "like a golf club". Having already operated on one hip, he wants to have a go at the other. Getting there and back is going to involve a lot of mileage: there's only a bed for one parent at a time, so we'll do daily swaps. I've delayed (yet again) taking part in the cannabis trial until it's over; driving while out of it isn't encouraged. So: Interferon, cannabis or Copaxone? London, Bury or Ipswich? All this decision-making makes my head spin. What I need is a neurologist.

Excerpt from 'A schoolboy error if ever there was one'
24 March 2002

Partly as a result of my multiple sclerosis and partly because of an operation my three-year old daughter needed, I've spent a lot of time in hospitals recently. They're pretty grim places generally, from the off-milk, cream paint on the walls to the strip lights suspended from those holes-like-Swiss-cheese ceiling tiles. It's all very 1940s, even down to the round pin-plugs halfway up the walls everywhere, next to those public information posters telling us to pack in the fags. But next time you're in, cast your eyes down. Look at the floor. Most hospitals lay down that skidmark-on-lino stuff. You know, the green or grey speckly plastic with a black smudge down it. But lino has a drawback, as I found out when I spilt a jug of water on the floor just before Martha's operation. It's slippery. After her slide, tumble and the ensuing banged head, we nearly had the operation cancelled.

So what's the alternative? Step forward those private-finance-initiative geniuses who – for a mere £210m – have built the new Royal Infirmary in Edinburgh. Their solution? Carpet. Lovely soft carpet. No chance of skidding on that. Unfortunately, there's not much chance of pushing a patient-laden trolley on it, either. Unless you're Geoff Capes, of course.

Introducing Me week

21 April 2002

I am not big on Days. Or Weeks for that matter. And particularly not Years. International Aids Day, Christian Aid Week, Breast Awareness Year. There seem to be a lot of them around just now, ensuring that we can feel guilty about our inaction all year round. To my mind, these are mostly just fundraising gimmicks, designed to catch the eye of bored news editors on slow days and then to lie forgotten for another 12 months.

But having said that, I should point out that today is MS Day, the culmination of MS Week, and that if you have a spare fiver left in your wallet this Sunda – despite Chancellor Brown's best efforts – then you could do a lot worse than to put it in an envelope and send it to the Multiple Sclerosis Society. You'll feel good. I may one day feel better, thanks to you.

Not least because MS is one area in which medical research is galloping ahead. So fast, in fact, that it could totally mess up the projections and assumptions of this week's Wanless Report, and the budget which followed. Even the Wanless Report's subtitle, "Taking a Long-Term View", implies that a seamless graph of NHS expenditure can be planned, with continued year-on-year boosts to the health budget. Not so. Mr Wanless recognises the potential problem. On page 127 of his report, he notes that: "The review recommends that further research is required in attempting to isolate the impact of technological change on health care spending." In other words: "I haven't got a clue what'll happen next."

On the day before Wanless was published, an American group of scientists announced initial findings which suggest that stem cell transplantation may well be helping some MS patients. If they're right, we're all going to want it. All 85,000 MS patients in the UK. How much is that going to cost, Derek? Medical breakthroughs tend to be both unpredictable and expensive. However much cash we throw at the NHS, however many committees are asked to look at future funding, these unpalatable prioritisations will have to be made. By elected politicians.

It has been announced this week that Prince William, undergraduate at St Andrews University, is planning to change courses in mid-stream, dumping his art history studies and switching to geography.

Now, speaking as one who also changed courses during my undistinguished university days, I am in no position to argue with our monarch-to-be's decision. But I am able to make a few suggestions. After all, as one of his future employers (ie, tax-paying subjects), I can warn him that his CV is unlikely to be enhanced by his choices.

First, the university itself. St Andrews has a reputation, you know. Those four -year courses, that faraway location. The whisper is, "St Andrews – a bit of a doss."

A doss is the relaxed and, frankly, slack university existence to which all Etonians aspire, but which employers frown upon.

Second, history of art. Got a bit of a Grand Tour, Sebastian Flyte cadence to it, hasn't it? A bit lolling-around-Florence-y? Not exactly horny-handed. So William has decided that it's not for him. But geography? Now, again, don't misunderstand. Some of my best friends did geography degrees. They tell me that its loads of work and doesn't just involve knowing the name of the longest river in Australia or the capital of Surinam. And I'm sure they're right (although their knowledge of things like that certainly comes in handy when assembling a well-rounded quiz team).

But I can't help thinking that William's intended career (Sovereign, Defender of the Faith etc) will hardly be helped by this addition. Even if is better than media studies, Edward.

Only a few months ago, the merry lads and laddesses at the Beeb were having a ritual laugh at those poor souls in the hideous aisles of commercial television. All those ads! The conventional wisdom, then, was that selling spots for chatlines and Bisto was guaranteed to switch viewers over, and ruin the pace of programmes.

All that has changed. Now, mainly thanks to the success of the episodic crime drama *24*, breaks are back in vogue. The word now is that regular breaks add momentum to programmes and help to pace productions, like chapters in a book.

So don't be surprised that when BBC2 decide to repeat 24 (as they surely will), they do so with the addition of multiple "pseudo-breaks" – trails, idents and the like – to inject that make-a-cuppa feeling.

Before I can get cannabis on the NHS, I'm made to remember shopping lists

12 May 2002

Sorry to disappoint all you dope smokers out there, but marijuana legalisation isn't something I get worked up about. If it's legalised, fine. If it isn't, so be it. So why was I sitting in the waiting room at the Institute of Neurology on Monday, desperately hoping that I'd get free dope from the cannabis-in-multiple sclerosis trial? I can tell you that it wasn't in the hope of getting a safe supply of Lebanese White Widow. It never did much for me.

Apparently cannabis helps some people with walking difficulties. And since this is a rather cheaper and safer method than a clandestine meeting with some spotty teenager with a Nirvana T-shirt in a Colchester subway, I joined the trial queue. Acquiring the weed this way isn't simple. First you have to be assessed. Hence last week's trip (pardon the pun) to Queen's Square in London's Bloomsbury. The Institute of Neurology is a bit swankier than the hospitals I've attended recently. It's got mosaics on the floor, and lurid portraits of the late Princess of Wales on the walls. First I had to see Emma the physiotherapist. Emma spent some time wiggling my arms and legs around, scoring my limbs for spasticity*. My right leg's a two, apparently. She was undecided about my left, but gave it a one. Whatever that means. Then it was time to see the doctor. He looked alarmingly younger than me – but then so does Carter in ER, and he's good, so I mustn't judge. Anyway, this doctor was called Rory, as is my one-year-old, so I gave him the benefit of the doubt.

Rory asked some questions, then gave me the verdict. "I'm delighted to tell you that you've been accepted for the trial." Delighted? So was I, actually. I don't think I could have stood the rejection.

So much for the good news. Now for the bad. "You understand that you can't go abroad while you're on the trial?"

"Abroad? No."

"We're going to provide you with sufficient quantity to merit arrest for intent to supply. I'll give you this card you can wave at any UK policeman - but it won't impress foreign cops." Great. Not that I have any plans to go abroad, mind. But the prospect of having my collar felt by a Turkish rozzer was depressing anyway. "And you can't drive either. I'm going to have to inform the Home Office of your intention to participate in the trial. If you crash a car while taking an illegal substance, that's a criminal offence."

So. No driving for three months. No foreign travel. David Blunkett gets a file on me. And the ordeal wasn't over yet. There was still the psychological test to endure.

Everyone knows that MS makes you fall over, bump into things and so on. But it can also make you a bit... you know... thingy... whatchemacallit... forgetful. And so can cannabis. Put the two together and what have you got? Where was I?

170

So the sadists at Queen's Square dreamt up a series of trials to test memory and speed of thinking. The first bit was a cinch – just a list of hard-to-pronounce words to read out. Even though I work for *The Independent on Sunday*, I don't use "demesne" very often, but it all seemed rather easy-peasy.

Then the test got harder. A tape was played, with a relentless list of numbers to add up. The tape went rather faster than my brain, and I think I flunked that one. Finally, the decider. A shopping list. I've always been bad at shopping lists. Even on a normal trip to Somerfield, I always forget something. Usually the cheese. That unforgiving glare from my wife as she unpacks... Oh God. And this list went on for ever. "Paprika, jacket, drill, parsley, vest..." I tried doing one of those mind maps you often read about in the silly season. A mental tour of Somerfield. (Paprika? It's by the Maldon salt.) But that didn't work because there were so many items that my local supermarket doesn't stock. They don't do jackets in Halstead Somerfield. By this time, the psychologist was at the end of the list. And she wanted me to repeat it. Five times. Images of my wife's scorning face shimmered in front of my eyes. I remembered about three items. And I haven't even started on the drugs yet.

* See Expanded Disability Status Scale in blog 44.

171

I'm just popping out to the chemist for my repeat prescription of cigarettes

9 June 2002

It's hardly surprising to me that Iain Duncan Smith is not having a great time as Tory leader. Using my infallible pick-a-winner method, I could have warned party members that Ken Clarke was the preferable choice. Nothing to do with the policies: just the habits. In a two-horse race, always plump for the smoker. For there's a secret, known only to us puffers, which colours this judgement. It is that smokers are Better People and More Interesting than our abstemious counterparts. In my opinion, you'll always find better conversations by the overflowing ashtray of the office smoking room, or among the huddled masses puffing out in the rain, than you will by the photocopier or the fax machine.

Now, don't get me wrong. I am quite aware that the above principle is utter tosh. But it's no more stupid than putting your faith in astrology, water-divining or Treasury models, and let's face it, lots of people believe in those. Secondly, I am entirely au fait with the downside of smoking: that it kills you. But hey, I've got multiple sclerosis, and that cuts your life expectancy too, by more than my daily intake of fags. Irritatingly, they don't tell you if these sentences are concurrent or consecutive – but let's assume that they cancel each other out, so those few tabs a day are a freebie for me.

Not that my wife sees it quite that way. Lucy discourages the habit. In our ashtray combat, she has two weapons at her disposal. The first is not my health – that's a lost caus – but our children's. On the unanswerable pretext of protecting Daisy, Martha and Rory from inhaling the toxic passive fumes, she has banned smoking anywhere in the house. Fair enough I suppose, and I have retreated to the shed with my stash of Silk Cut.

So now she has a new argument. Money. Thanks to successive chancellors (including the traitorous Ken Clarke), cigarettes are extremely expensive: £4.50 for a pack of 20. That's 22p each. (Oh for the days when an illicit pack was less than a quid at Windsor Riverside Railway Station). It mounts up. To prove that my intake is unaffordable, Lucy has started to scribble down monthly budgets under which no money is left over for fripperies, ie fags. It's all there: everything in, everything out. And it adds up to zero. In the starkest terms, it's either cigs for me or new shoes for the girls.

So now it's my turn for a fightback. We may not be able to afford packs, OK. But how about roll-ups? They're much cheaper. Hitherto, there has been a fatal flaw in this argument: I can't roll my own. All attempts I've made in the past have resulted in an empty Rizla paper stuck to my bottom lip. Hopeless. And not very tasty either. But there's a new thingy, tailor-made for broke tobacco addicts with MS. It stuffs ready-rolled tubes with tobacco. Not perfectly maybe, but better than anything I can do. The result even looks like a real cigarette, even when I put cannabis in it to help the walking (I deferred the NHS trial last week because I need to drive).

So now the real challenge begins: getting tobacco on the NHS. Not very likely, you might think. In the past, those killjoy doctors have rather frowned on smokers. But maybe the department can make an exception in this case. After all, Health Secretary Alan Milburn's clinical excellence committee, Nice, has spent much of the past year trying to persuade those of us on expensive disease-modifying MS drugs that the NHS can't afford to stump up the £7,000 per patient per year that they cost. Well here's a wheeze for you, Al. Free rolling tobacco for all MS patients! Relatively cheap, easier to administer than those fiddly injections every day and – you never know your luck – it could help to get us off your hands that bit sooner.

Set up yet another task force, Al: put Ken Clarke on to the idea. And get one of Stephen Byers' old spin doctors to make the announcement at a "good time" – like the outbreak of World War Three in Kashmir or when England get booted out by Denmark in the second round of the World Cup.

What do I have to do to get my hands on some really good drugs?

14 July 2002

The new BMA president, Sir Anthony Grabham, was widely applauded for a speech recently in which he described the "Third World" state of much of our healthcare. In fact, judging by my experience over the past month, he was unduly kind. Third World healthcare is much more civilised.

On hearing of my multiple sclerosis these days, most people come up with a similar line which I must have heard 100 times; something like: "Well, at least you're getting those drugs free on the NHS nowadays." So, in the week that I've just paid yet another five hundred quid for one month's supply, let me tell you that, in this new "patient-centred NHS", it's not quite as simple as that.

It is true that Alan Milburn's department issued a directive earlier this year that Beta Interferon and Copaxone (my one) should be available for prescription in the spring. It's true, too, that I've spoken to my GP, my NHS neurologist, the head of the local Primary Care Trust, even to the drug suppliers and manufacturers. All are happy – or at least willing – to provide me with the potions. I've had the NHS prescription written, I've sent it off to the suppliers. I've waited. I've rung. I've emailed. But – no drugs. Now, listen carefully; not even Franz Kafka came up with a bureaucracy as spookily arcane as this. Even though my care trust here in Essex has agreed to pay, it appears that the initial cash needs to come from Bart's Trust in London. And some pharmacist at Bart's has put a stop on the prescription because, even though it was ordered to prescribe by the Department of Health, the London-based Barking Primary Care Trust hasn't yet had its meeting at which the funding is to be agreed (Bart's comes within its area, believe it or not). It's scheduled for some time this month.

What the hell is going on with the NHS when some bastard from Barking can stop me getting the drugs which my GP and my neurologist think I need – and my local trust will cough up for? My sister's old boss, Nicholas Soames, kindly even put down a couple of Parliamentary Questions about the problem. The answer to the first was quick and concise. Minister Hazel Blears wrote to him that "Copaxone is available on the NHS under the risk-sharing scheme for disease-modifying drugs for multiple sclerosis that came into operation on 6 May 2002". Clear, swift – and no help at all. For the minister chose not to answer, yet, the second question: "To ask the Secretary of State for Health if Copaxone is available at St Batholomew's Hospital; and for what reasons a valid prescription for Copaxone would be inadmissible." You might think that one hard to evade, but following last week's revelations from the Lib Dems about just how sneakily civil servants try to avoid straight questions, I've looked for the flaw in this one. And I'm afraid I've found it. You see, my prescription did not come from Bart's itself – it came from the London, another hospital in Bart's Trust. So I fully expect more flannel, more waiting, more frustration.

A year or so ago I described the desperation among MS sufferers like me for a big name to come down with our disease. Not that I wish it on any of them, but it would certainly be handy if we could garner a bit of the "sexy" cachet that Michael J Fox,

174

Muhammed Ali and even Ronald Reagan have given to Alzheimer's and Parkinson's. Why can't we bag a big-name victim?

Well, now we have. The biggest of them all. Potus himself. For the uninitiated, that means the President of the United States. Yes, that finger on the nuclear button could well have a worrisome shake, as Josiah Bartlett reaches out towards all our annihilations. Josiah who?, you may ask. I'm afraid that's the problem. Its not the real Potus, that gurning goof from Texas. It's just the pretend one portrayed by Martin Sheen in Channel 4's *The West Wing* who's got the disease. OK, so he looks a bit like JFK – they've even got that Kennedyesque photo from behind in the opening titles. But he's not real. He's bull.

Rather like those free drugs we all heard so much about.

The hole in my back tooth and my MS: are they in some way related?

8 September 2002

In a report last week, the Medical Research Council called for yet more research (and therefore more lovely funding, I guess) to assess properly the effects of adding fluoride to Britain's water supply. There's so much fluoride in toothpaste, it wails, that proper benchmarks are hard to lay down.

All of which will be grist to the mill of the Green Ink Brigade, that doughty band of Conspiracy Theorist letter writers who blame compulsory water fluoridation for everything from the Kennedy Assassination to Sophie Wessex's wardrobe disasters.

Up here in the remoter parts of Essex, we're on our own water supply, so I don't get anything put in my drinks. But I've another dilemma just now, which will excite the Green Inkers. Fillings.

Personally, I blame the confectionery-industrial complex. I mean, how can anyone be expected to resist a Highland toffee? So hard, so pliable to the suck, so yummy. But there's a price to pay, and it's sitting right in front of me. A filling fell out last week. Must be the third this year. And I haven't been to the dentist yet for any of them.

Looking at this lumpy piece of amalgam, I can't even work out which way it's supposed to go back in, so I guess I'll have to suffer the stripy fish and plastic shipwreck in the gloomy tank, and the old copies of Yachting Monthly, on offer at the dentists. I'm not filled with terror at the prospect: needles and syringes are pretty commonplace to me – after all, I have to give myself a jab every day already. And all those white coats and pink liquids are reassuringly pseudo-medical. But the question remains: what do I get to replace the missing metal?

Now I could just ask them to put new amalgam in the holes. But there's another option, urged by quasi-scientific multiple-sclerosis gurus and Conspiracy Theorists: getting new white fillings instead. The logic for this is something to do with amalgam incorporating mercury, the fumes of which are bad news or something. The exact link between this and MS is a bit fuzzy, but hey – it's all good revenue for the Conspiracists (and the dentists.)

There's no shortage of alarming statistics, particularly now that the internet can bring the horrors of "mercury toxicity" or "negative electrical current" direct to your desktop. But is it all bollocks?

I'm no scientist, but, armed only with my trusty O-levels in chemistry and physics, I can assert that it is. "Negative electrical current" sounds like Star Trek guff, and as to being poisoned by mercury, I reckon I had some symptoms of this MS back in the days when I foolishly boasted of being filling-free.

But what makes it all so attractive, I guess, is that blaming somebody – your dentist, the military, the water tamperers, whoever – gives you a villain for your misfortune. Every effect has a cause, we learn at school. So what's the cause of my MS? Or for energetic five-year-olds dying of meningitis? Or for apparently random strokes, for that matter? Of course, when we ask these questions, we don't really want to know the causes – which are always some impenetrable platitude about immune systems and genetics. What we want is reasons. And, except for the hyper-religious among us, some bloke in a black dress spouting gobbledegook about merciful God seeing every little sparrow fall is cold comfort. Because the reason is: there is no reason. It's all so damn unfair ... but life's like that. If only the religious and the Conspiracy Theorists could see this, we wouldn't hear their nonsense on Thought for the Day or read it in green ink.

None of which goes any way towards helping me with my filling dilemma. I recognise that the amalgam-is-poison debate is drivel, but those white ones are better to look at. And isn't it best to be on the safe side? In this case, no. The fillings are at the back, so nobody will see them anyway. Amalgam is cheap, and you can't get white stuff on the NHS. Plus those Green Inkers are out to get m – to switch. That's the clincher.

So MS is sexually transmitted, is it? Just look at me and you'll know it's a lie

21 September 2002

Lock up your daughters. The sex god is back in town. A report out last week – citing a Danish study, no less – suggests that multiple sclerosis, the disease I've got, could be sexually transmitted. And that surely means that I must be a bit of a dude between the sheets (know what I mean, nudge, nudge?)

In the current issue of the Journal of Neurology, Neurosurgery and Psychiatry, a paper suggests that MS is more common in sexually permissive societies, and that incidence of the disease increased around the time that the contraceptive pill became available. Not only that, the study notes that the arrival of 20,000 young, strapping (no doubt sex-starved) British troops in Orkney and Shetland between 1954 and 1974 led to a four-fold increase in the incidence of MS. Surely that clinches it?

I'm afraid not. Tempting as it may be to equate one's own disease with sexual adventurousness, I'm afraid that the facts don't support the theory. If I were to follow Tracey Emin's example – inscribing all my sex partners on a duvet – the result would hardly cover my feet. Even then, I'd have to sew large letters. Not only can I count my sex partners on the fingers of one hand – I can count them on the fingers of one of Bart Simpson's hands. But the report doesn't end with its suggestion that adult MS may be linked to youthful promiscuity. Most unpleasantly, the report implies that child sex abuse may be the root cause of MS in children and young women.

Now, I haven't studied the relationship between child abuse and MS, so it ill behoves me to suggest that there is no link – although I can certainly attest that there's none in my case. But it strikes me that the report's author, Dr Christopher Hawkes, has not done his homework either. There isn't anything in the report to suggest – to take just one rather obvious example – that any research has been done on the incidence of child abuse among MS patients compared to the general population, nor even that his theory has undergone the normal process of peer review: the Journal boasts of its new internet-based review system, which is bound to be open to abuse.

Nevertheless, Dr Hawkes feels sufficiently confident of his theory to posit, somewhat pompously, "I propose that multiple sclerosis is a sexually transmitted infection acquired principally during adolescence".

Like spying witches in Tudor times, whose innocence could only be proven by drowning, accusations of child abuse are the touchstone allegation of our age. Since it is almost impossible to convince the finger-pointers that one has not been abused ("you've just repressed the memory, you poor thing"), child abuse has become the easiest allegation to make – and the hardest to shrug off.

Now I'm not suggesting that allegations of child abuse should be generally ignored, nor that they are invariably untrue. Five minutes spent studying the transcripts of the Victoria Climbié inquiry should be enough to convince anyone that not only is child abuse real – but that it is just as horrific as any number of NSPCC advertisements would have you believe.

No, what I'm arguing for is the opposite. It is because child abuse is real, and because its effects are so horrific, that perhaps a bit more caution should be shown before bandying the accusation around too freely.

Neither would I do anything other than welcome serious study into the causes of multiple sclerosis. It is a horrible, degenerative disease which affects too many. And if child abuse, tooth-filling amalgam or even childhood overcleanliness – each of which has been blamed at one time or another – turns out to be a significant cause, then I look forward to reading the proof.

But if – as I suspect is rather more likely – the root cause of this illness turns out to be messier, less clear-cut, more to do with genetics and proteins than these easy answers suggest – then I hope that Dr Hawes and his drivel-peddling colleagues will be prepared to accept this evidence, and crack on with finding a cure.

I can cut out the fags. I can cast out 'Big Brother'. But I can't stop the shakes

1 December 2002

Today, November is over, which may mean little to you, but it is a godsend to me. It means that my bet with my wife is over, and I can smugly light up cigarettes again. Perplexing as it may seem, giving up smoking – for a one-month period only – is actually quite a doddle for me. I don't get withdrawal symptoms, don't go into cold turkey. It's just rather boring. So I'm glad that the bet has been won: a few fags give a structure to my day.

Which may seem reason enough for cheer this morning – but I'm nevertheless feeling rather bereft. One of my habits has returned, but the other one is gone for another twelvemonth. Yes, Celebrity Big Brother has ended, with the victor, ex-Take That ter Mark Owen, walking off with the title (opening a superstore near you soon). To mollify the many critics of CBB2 – not least last year's champion Jack Dee, who said: "I wish Big Brother would just curl up and die"– I will admit that there were some dreadful flaws in this year's series. The housemates all seemed to get on rather too well – we could have done with a bit more grit. Then, there was the dysfunction between different levels of fame. For some of the housemates – notably Anne Diamond – the appearance on CBB will hardly merit a mention on the cv: far more famous exhibitions will take pride of place. For other – most obviously Sue Perkins (from comedy duo Mel and Sue) – this was the centrepice of their career to date. As such, players like Sue seemed increasingly desperate to win the game, picking on rivals like Richard-Branson-with-unfeasibly-large-falsies lookalike Melinda Messenger. Sue's tactics were misguided anyway, confusing the survivor of CBB with the winner. They are not the same: last year Jack Dee may have remained the longest in the house, but it was Claire Sweeney who took the honours – by dint of being nice about her housemates.

But my love-in with Big Brother, even my addiction to fags, can be overcome. I'll miss the housemates, sure. But I can handle it. There is, however, one habit I can't kick, even though I'd rather like

Anyone who watched the Parkinsonian Muhammad Ali – hands shaking all over the place – try to light the Atlanta Olympic flame, knows what an irritating symptom tremor can be, for both victim and, frankly, for the viewer. Go on, Muhammad, fire that arrow. I've not got it as bad as the ex-heavyweight. Anyway, nobody's likely to ask me to perform a pointless feat of archery in front of the watching billions. But still my left arm wobbles in an alarming (to others) and tiring (to me) way. This is not – not yet, anyway – as disruptive to my daily life as it might be, even though I'm left-handed. For a start, this is not the type of tremor which gets worse when I try to do things. Nor is it even completely uncontrollable: if I focus hard enough, I can even stop it for a while. But it is a nuisance: who wants to concentrate on their shaky hand all day? No, don't answer that. And even though the tremor doesn't bother me that much, it certainly affects how others react towards me. Other symptoms of MS – dizziness, falling over, erratic eyesight etc – are much more disruptive to me. But to the observer, they just look like I've had a few too many at an early office Christmas party. Whereas, the shakes? That's a proper cripple's symptom. When my tremor's playing havoc, everyone leaps up to offer me a seat on crowded commuter trains. Even the beggars avoid me.

And that's a problem. Just as concentration on controlling the shakes can switch the tremor off, so standing on a train and wishing-I-had-a-tremor-cos-then-those-bastards-would-offer-me-a-place-to-sit can switch it on. Which may be convenient for getting me a chair, but once the tremor has started, it's gonna be there all day. So, best not to think about it. Have a fag. At least the next series of 24 will be on soon.

Severe and acute flu? My Ars!

13 April 2003

Taxonomy, it's called. The science of naming things. Noah had it pretty easy compared to today's taxonomists. Yes, legend tells that he had to give labels to each of the two-by-two species on the ark – but at least he had only his eyesight to distinguish one animal from another. Today, electron microscopes and million-dollar laboratories allow men in white coats to make ever finer distinctions between the billions of bugs, beetles, lizards and leaves that need codifying. Meanwhile they have to rely on an ever dwindling supply of names.

It's a similar situation with diseases. Now we've got a new one to worry about. Sars, the fatal new Hong Kong flu. Severe Acute Respiratory Syndrome. Now where did that name come from? In my dictionary, "Severe" and "Acute" mean the same thing. After all, is there such a thing as Severe Mild Respiratory Syndrome? I think not.

No, what I believe is that the taxonomists got in a huddle. "Acute Respiratory Syndrome!" someone suggested. That prompted nods from the assembly. But one objection came. "That won't do. Who wants to get a thing called ARS?"

Severe Respiratory Syndrome was ruled out too. Vowel-less acronyms such as SRS don't trip off the tongue, and in these post-Aids days, everyone wants a good acronym for their illness. So Sars it is.

I mention this disease-acronym obsession because it's affecting me this week. Take my affliction, MS. It used to be called Disseminating Sclerosis, but I suppose that DS didn't sound so good. But MS sounds a bit like ME – and that's been causing me some confusion recently.

"MS? Isn't that like yuppie flu?" they ask, innocently.

"Yuppie flu? No, it bloody isn't!" I snap back.

It's bad enough to have a disease – but it's worse when people mix up your thing with something that they don't really believe exists. Now, I don't want to pick a fight with ME sufferers. They'll doubtless deluge me with mail otherwise. Assuming they've got the energy. So I'm well prepared to state that I'm sure they've got a real affliction, and I'm sure it's horrible, painful, uncomfortable etc, etc. I just wish that their illness had a different name, that's all.

You see, it's rarely spoken of, but there's a mental hierarchy of disease. Having MS is a bit like being middle class. Like Ronnie Barker in that Frost Report sketch, we can look down on the commoner ailments and patronise people with colds or ingrowing toenails: "Oh, poor you, that must be awful. Sounds really nasty." But at the same time, we're looked down upon by the real sufferers. Aids, cancer, flesh-eating bugs... You've gotta respect people with one of those.

And then there are the undefinable ones, like ME. Is it a proper middle – class disease – or a poor man's (or, more usually, a rich woman's) excuse?

All of which matters, because it has dramatic effects on money-raising. Today is the last day of MS week, timed to hit the London Marathon and all that vital sponsorship for the MS Society. My heartfelt thanks to all of those who are raising money to find a cure today. But look around at all the other worthy causes vying for your attention – and your cash. Pink and red ribbons will be everywhere, as misery branding goes global. If you find yourself in the capital today, you might even want to wend your way up to Tottenham Court Road. Doubtless this morning, like most days, there are bucket shakers vying for your spare change for their chosen cause. But have they got a sexy acronym of a name? If so, their collecting pots are probably stuffed with cash already. I'd recommend saving your dough for the less fortunate.

Once upon a time, these things counted for naught. Charities were often founded with the name of their chairmen: Leonard Cheshire, Sue Ryder – that sort of thing. But these names, evoking a long-lost era, must now be something of a millstone for charities trying to portray themselves as modern, forward-thinking, third millennium. Hence the Spastics Society's need to rename itself as Scope. Make no mistake, in this game, names matter. Send for the taxonomists.

As an MS sufferer, this verdict makes my life a little more bearable
Comment

31 July 2009

First things first: I have no intention whatsoever of buying a one-way ticket to Switzerland. Not now and, hopefully, not ever: my multiple sclerosis is quite manageable at the moment, thank you.

As it is for millions. The variety of symptoms and degree of incapacity in MS are enormous. There are plenty of people with MS with no visible symptoms whatsoever. Then again, there are those living with some of the most ghastly afflictions imaginable: blindness, spasticity, inability to talk or swallow and, of course, pain. Some 15 per cent of MS sufferers commit suicide. And helping the sufferer on their way is illegal.

As it stands, the law seems clear enough. It is illegal – with up to 14 years in jail if found guilty – to counsel, procure, aid or abet a suicide. But the devil is in the detail: what does it mean to aid and abet? Is pushing a wheelchair an illegal act? Buying a map?

And so the news of Debbie Purdy's success in prompting the law lords to instruct the DPP to clarify the law on assisted suicide has reignited the debate among those of us with nasty diseases about the rights and wrongs of ending what may – and I repeat may – become an unendurable existence.

For many with MS, this debate is one best left under the carpet. There has never yet been a prosecution for any family member taking the trip to Dignitas, they point out. So why drag out the dirty linen? For such people, Debbie Purdy is a useful idiot, cynically manoeuvred by the suicide lobby. How would we feel, they ask, if the case had been brought not by Ms Purdy herself, but by her husband, Omar Puente?

It so happens that, in my day job, I've met both Ms Purdy and Mr Puente. As the producer of Sir David Frost's programme for Al Jazeera English, *Frost Over The World*, I invited Debbie and Omar to the studio earlier this year. As an MS patient quite content to put off any thoughts of Swiss travel, I was keen to find out why she is forcing us to think about things we'd rather not consider.

"We've been married for 10 years; we've been together for 13. I love him and I wouldn't want to be the cause of him putting himself in harm's way as far as the legal system is concerned," she said.

If her MS worsens, she argued, she would be tempted to make the trip to Switzerland alone, before the symptoms become unendurable – rather than wait until she became completely incapacitated and unable to travel without Omar.

I fully accept that for many MS patients – many with symptoms far worse than mine – Debbie Purdy's triumph with the law lords this week was an unwelcome and inappropriate intervention – like a loud fart at a Buckingham Palace tea party. But the overriding symptom of MS is uncertainty: you never know when you might have to face the nasty decisions. And, unpleasant though it might be, the law lords and Debbie Purdy have, for many of us, made it just a bit more bearable.

My farewell to Al Jazeera

Think (issue 4) 2013

Some seven years ago, when Al Jazeera launched an English version and decided to make some programs in London, it was too good an opportunity to miss. I was at the time the television critic for a UK newspaper, so I bid farewell to writing about good to indifferent TV, and made some instead. As producer of a weekly hour, Frost Over the World, I was able to boss people about, saying how things should be done in front of a camera, and in particular how to do interviews – without ever having had to do it myself. Except once. And it's not an experience I want to repeat.

Back in the 1980s, the then editor of a current affairs series I was working on made a habit of always dressing immaculately on program day. His hair was washed, his shirt pressed, his suit dry-cleaned. Perplexed, I asked him why he bothered. "Ah," he told me. "It's in case your presenter doesn't turn up and you have to present the program yourself instead. Always wear a smart suit on program day." Good advice. Which I ignored.

And so it was, one fateful day. A guest – the novelist Ian McEwan* – in the Green Room, and a presenter irreversibly delayed, with no prospect of him turning up any time soon, and no replacement to hand. And me looking like a roadie for some obscure Belgian combo. Plus, I hadn't read any of his novels since university. I hadn't even seen the movie Atonement.

There wasn't much choice, and McEwan was a sweetheart about being interviewed by an idiot. We managed eight minutes or so. But never again will I believe that presenting TV is a doddle. Until that day, Al Jazeera had welcomed any YouTube comments about their programs. But so vituperative – and so voluminous – were the hostile words about my hair, my clothes, my speech, etc, that comments were thenceforward discontinued.

Arguably the biggest advantage of working for Al Jazeera is that, unlike the domestic networks I produced for before, they don't collect viewing figures, so we never had a clue how many people were watching our stuff, which is a massive liberation for program makers. Neither did they, contrary to what everyone seems to assume, interfere unduly with our editorial independence, so for years I was able to do pretty much whatever I wanted. And, of course, they had the funds for us to do things almost instantly, things that would have taken months to set up when I'd been at the BBC.

I remember about three years ago getting a call on a Monday from the vice-president of somewhereland, saying that he was doing some pretty interesting election-monitoring that week in a remote part of Paraguay, and would we like to interview him about it? Two days later, a satellite truck had been dispatched to a village north of Asuncion and we were talking, live, to this vice-president chap about some voting shenanigans he'd seen. To be honest, it may have been pretty dull. Vice-presidents often are. But it was magnificent too.

However, a Qatar-based channel can only, I guess, be expected to make programs in the UK for so long, and after seven years they have decided to base all future programs in Doha. Bad luck for me, as the multiple sclerosis I've got tends to deteriorate in hot weather. I fall over even more often in Doha than I do in Colchester, in eastern England. I even fell into a gorse-filled ditch in East Timor on a recent trip, so a move to Doha is a no-no for me. Added to all that, we've got a house move imminent.

Living, as we've done for the past 15 years, out in the sticks – a 25-minute drive from the nearest railway station – I really need a car to get about, and (as my wife never tires of telling me), I'm a terrible driver even without the MS. The government agency that issues them may well confiscate my driving license next year, so we are moving to Cambridge, where I can catch a bus to the station if needed. And I must watch Atonement in the Arts Picturehouse. You never know...

This article was originally published in Think (issue 4) in 2013 and is reprinted here by kind permission of the Qatar Foundation.

* See blog 101

The pug lover

Charlie and Bob in Glenelg, August 1994

After Charlie died, his sister, Candy, wrote to John Hegley, also a lover of pugs and he very kindly wrote a poem in Charlie's honour, that was read at Charlie's thanksgiving service. When I wrote to John again, to ask if I could print the poem in this book, this was his reply:

Dear Lucy,

It sounds an exciting prospect, getting Charlie's blog further 'out there'. In terms of the poem, please feel free to use it in any way you wish and to donate any proceeds, again as you see fit.

I've just been reading the part in the blog about senses working overtime and Charlie not being able to smell the flower that only blooms once in 100 years. It is an important passage which makes us value senses we have.

As you have sensed, his blog is a value to the world.

John

A piece of puggetry for Charlie

There's pegs for clothing, clogs for feet
there's trotty pigs and what a treat
to have all these and pugs as well:
a softness needing no hard-sell.

Audacious humans hog the news,
but have they dug the nacious pugaroos?
There's biz that is not brotherly.
There's cataclysmic disagreements.
There's uglinesses to be found;
there's less when there are pugs around.

A poetry with pride of pugs
is Paganini to the lugs.
A man called Prince could play and sing,
but with no pug,
he was not king.

John Hegley, February 2016

Thank you to Sally Alexander, Angela Burton, Sholto Byrnes, Edward Cappabianca, David Dimbleby, Debra King, Sue Douglas, Sean O'Grady, John Hegley, *The Independent*, Diana Muir, Katherine Porter and all at Whitefox Publishing.

Some of the proceeds from this book will be donated to the Multiple Sclerosis International Federation.

Lightning Source UK Ltd.
Milton Keynes UK
UKOW07f0227200217
294801UK00009B/33/P